Combo Sp... S0-APM-497 ...3A

World Link | Developing English Fluency

Susan Stempleski

James R. Morgan • Nancy Douglas

HEINLE
CENGAGE Learning™

Australia • Brazil • Japan • Korea • Mexico • Singapore • Spain • United Kingdom • United States

HEINLE
CENGAGE Learning

World Link, **Combo Split 3A**
Susan Stempleski
James R. Morgan, Nancy Douglas

Publisher: Christopher Wenger
Director of Content Development:
Anita Raducanu
Director of Product Marketing: Amy Mabley
Acquisitions Editor: Mary Sutton-Paul
Sr. Marketing Manager: Eric Bredenberg
Developmental Editor: Paul MacIntyre
Content Project Manager: Tan Jin Hock
Sr. Print Buyer: Mary Beth Hennebury
Compositor: CHROME Media Pte. Ltd.
Project Manager: Christopher Hanzie
Photo Researcher: Christopher Hanzie
Illustrator: Raketshop Design Studio
(Philippines)
Cover/Text Designer: CHROME Media Pte. Ltd.
Cover Images: CHROME Media Pte. Ltd.
PhotoDisc, Inc.

Photo Credits
Unless otherwise stated, all photos are from PhotoDisc, Inc. Digital Imagery © copyright 2005 PhotoDisc, Inc. and TYA Inc. Photos from other sources: page 6 (left) Yuriko Nakao/Reuters/Landov, (middle) Axel Seidemann/Bloomberg News/Landov, (right) Reuters/CORBIS; page 9: (top left) MPI/Getty Images, (bottom left) Directphoto/Alamy; page 11: (bottom left) Charles & Josette Lenars/CORBIS, (bottom right) Randy Faris/CORBIS; page 12: (far right) DAJ/Digital Images; page 18: (left) Peter Turnley/CORBIS, (right) Akio Suga/EPA/Landov; page 21: (left) Gustau Nacarino/Reuters/Landov; page 23: (left) Gregory Pace/CORBIS, (right) Reuters/Landov; page 31: Wenn/Landov; page 36: (D. Beckham) Kieran Doharty/Reuters/CORBIS, (J. Simpson) Fred Prouser/Reuters/Landov, (Madonna) Fred Prouser/Reuters/Landov, (S. Austin) Azzara Steve/CORBIS SYGMA, (L. Liu) Reuters/CORBIS; page 37: Reuters/Landov; page 42: (bottom) MAPS.com/CORBIS; page 47: (top) David Muench/CORBIS; page 50: (left) Russell Underwood/CORBIS, (right) Anders Ryman/CORBIS; page 59: (top) Jens Kalaene/dpa/Landov, (bottom) Ed Kashi/CORBIS; page 62: (top all) C. Hanzie/CHROME Media Pte Ltd, (bottom) CORBIS; page 69: (bottom left) C. Hanzie/CHROME Media Pte Ltd

Every effort has been made to trace all sources of illustrations/photos/information in this book, but if any have been inadvertently overlooked, the publisher will be pleased to make the necessary arrangements at the first opportunity.

ISBN-13: 978-1-4130-1086-2

ISBN-10: 1-4130-1086-5

Heinle
25 Thomson Place
Boston, Massachusetts 02210
USA

Cengage Learning is a leading provider of customized learning solutions with office locations around the globe, including Singapore, the United Kingdom, Australia, Mexico, Brazil and Japan. Locate our local office at:
international.cengage.com/region

Cengage Learning products are represented in Canada by Nelson Education, Ltd.

Visit Heinle online at **elt.heinle.com**
Visit our corporate website at **cengage.com**

Printed in China by China Translation & Printing Services Limited
4 5 6 7 8 9 10 12 10 09

Acknowledgments

We would firstly like to thank the educators who provided invaluable feedback throughout the development of the *World Link* series:

Byung-kyoo Ahn, Chonnam National University; Elisabeth Blom, Casa Thomas Jefferson; Grazyna Anna Bonomi; Vera Burlamaqui Bradford, Instituto Brasil-Estados Unidos; Araceli Cabanillas Carrasco, Universidad Autónoma de Sinaloa; Silvania Capua Carvalho, State University of Feira de Santana; Tânia Branco Cavaignac, Casa Branca Idiomas; Kyung-whan Cha, Chung-Ang University; Chwun-li Chen, Shih Chien University; María Teresa Fátima Encinas, Universidad Iberoamericana-Puebla and Universidad Autónoma de Puebla; Sandra Gaviria, Universidad EAFIT; Marina González, Instituto de Lenguas Modernas; Frank Graziani, Tokai University; Chi-ying Fione Huang, Ming Chuan University; Shu-fen Huang (Jessie), Chung Hua University; Tsai, Shwu Hui (Ellen), Chung Kuo Institute of Technology and Commerce; Connie R. Johnson, Universidad de las Américas-Puebla; Diana Jones, Instituto Angloamericano; Annette Kaye, Kyoritsu Women's University; Lee, Kil-ryoung, Yeungnam University; David Kluge, Kinjo Gakuin University; Nancy H. Lake; Hyunoo Lee, Inha University; Amy Peijung Lee, Hsuan Chuang College; Hsiu-Yun Liao, Chinese Culture University; Yuh-Huey Gladys Lin, Chung Hua University; Eleanor Occeña, Universitaria de Idiomas, Universidad Autónoma del Estado de Hidalgo; Laura Pérez Palacio, Tecnológico de Monterrey; Doraci Perez Mak, União Cultural Brasil-Estados Unidos; Mae-Ran Park, Pukyong National University; Joo-Kyung Park, Honam University; Bill Pellowe, Kinki University; Margareth Perucci, Sociedade Brasileira de Cultura Inglesa; Nevitt Reagan, Kansai Gaidai University; Lesley D. Riley, Kanazawa Institute of Technology; Ramiro Luna Rivera, Tecnológico de Monterrey, Prepa; Marie Adele Ryan, Associação Alumni; Michael Shawback, Ritsumeikan University; Kathryn Singh, ITESM; Grant Trew, Nova Group; Michael Wu, Chung Hua University

---

A great many people participated in the making of the *World Link* series. In particular I would like to thank the authors, Nancy Douglas and James Morgan, for all their hard work, creativity, and good humor. I would also like to give special thanks to the developmental editor Paul MacIntyre, whose good judgment and careful attention to detail were invaluable. Thanks, too, to publisher Chris Wenger, and all the other wonderful people at Heinle who have worked on this project. I am also very grateful to the many reviewers around the world, whose insightful comments on early drafts of the *World Link* materials were much appreciated.
Susan Stempleski

We'd like to extend a very special thank you to two individuals at Heinle: Chris Wenger for spearheading the project and providing leadership, support and guidance throughout the development of the series, and Paul MacIntyre for his detailed and insightful editing, and his tireless commitment to this project. We also offer our sincere thanks to Susan Stempleski, whose extensive experience and invaluable feedback helped to shape the material in this book.

Thanks also go to those on the editorial, production, and support teams who helped to make this book happen: Anita Raducanu, Sally Cogliano, David Bohlke, Christine Galvin-Combet, Lisa Geraghty, Carmen Corral-Reid, Jean Pender, Rebecca Klevberg, Mary Sutton-Paul, and their colleagues in Asia and Latin America.

I would also like to thank my parents, Alexander and Patricia, for their love and encouragement. And to my husband Jorge and daughter Jasmine—thank you for your patience and faith in me. I couldn't have done this without you!
Nancy Douglas

I would also like to thank my mother, Frances P. Morgan, for her unflagging support and my father, Lee Morgan Jr., for instilling the love of language and learning in me.
James R. Morgan

Reading & Writing	Language Link	Communication

Indoors and Outdoors

Lesson A | At home

1 Vocabulary Link

Around the house

A Match the words on the left with those on the right to make the names of eleven things commonly found in the home.

___ 1. air	a. alarm
___ 2. barbecue	b. cleaner
___ 3. alarm	c. clock
___ 4. burglar	d. conditioner
___ 5. can	e. control
___ 6. frying	f. detector
___ 7. remote	g. grill
___ 8. smoke	h. machine
___ 9. swimming	i. opener
___ 10. vacuum	j. pan
___ 11. washing	k. pool

B Pair work. Match ten of the items above to their pictures below.

ask& ANSWER

How many of the items above are in your home? Where are they usually kept? Which items are necessary? Which are luxury items?

2 Listening

A vacation home

 A Carson and Jenna are looking for a vacation rental home. Listen. Circle the one they choose.
(CD 1, Track 1)

1.

2.

B Listen again. Write 1 if the sentence describes the first place.
Write 2 if it describes the second place. (CD 1, Track 2)

1. It's in a cooler area. ____

2. It has a washing machine. ____

3. It doesn't have an air conditioner. ____

4. It's near the ocean. ____

5. You can't watch TV here. ____

6. You don't have to pack a lot to stay here. ____

7. Jenna likes it. ____

8. There's a lot of fresh fruit here. ____

3 Pronunciation

Plural endings /s/, /z/, and /ɪz/

ask&
ANSWER

When you go on vacation, which do you prefer: a simple place with few luxuries or a fully furnished luxury place? Why?

 A Listen to the plural endings of the underlined nouns.
Notice how each ending is pronounced differently. (CD 1, Track 3)

1. Does that store sell alarm clocks? /s/

2. The club has two swimming pools. /z/

3. I broke several dishes. /ɪz/

 B Listen to these sentences. Notice the plural endings of the underlined words. Then listen again and check the pronunciation you hear for each ending. (CD 1, Track 4)

	/s/	/z/	/ɪz/
1. They don't have any vacuum cleaners.	☐	☐	☐
2. Please close the curtains.	☐	☐	☐
3. He washed all the cups.	☐	☐	☐
4. She sold two houses last week.	☐	☐	☐
5. Did you water the plants?	☐	☐	☐
6. My family has two antique dressers.	☐	☐	☐

Lesson A • At home   **3**

4 Speaking

I need a place for my tools.

A Andy is thinking about buying a house. Marcus is showing him the house. Listen and underline the words used to describe the house. (CD 1, Track 5)

Marcus: This is the living room.

Andy: It's nice and roomy.

Marcus: Yes. There's a lot of room. It's a two-bedroom house. One bedroom is upstairs.

Andy: I see. What's that building?

Marcus: That's a shed. It's used for storing tools.

Andy: Great. I like to garden. I need a place for my tools.

Marcus: That's good. Shall we go outside and look at the backyard?

Andy: OK!

B Pair work. Practice the conversation with a partner.

ask&
ANSWER
What features do you think are important in a new home?

5 Speaking Strategy

Saying what you want

A Look at these three different kinds of housing. Check (✓) the one(s) you would like to live in. You can also add other types of housing on the lines below.

 houseboat

high-rise condominium

ranch house

Other types of housing: _____

_____

B Group work. Discuss your choices with your group members. Be sure to explain your reasons.

I need a lot of space. I chose the ranch house.

Really? I'd like to live on the houseboat. It sounds fun.

Useful Expressions:
Saying what you want

I need a lot of space.

I want to live on a houseboat.

I'd like/love to have a house with 20 rooms.

6 Language Link

Describing use: *be used* + infinitive; *be used for* + gerund or noun

A Study the chart. Notice the prepositions in italics and the words that follow them.

A lawn mower is used . . .	*to* cut grass.	(infinitive)
	for cutting grass.	(*for* + gerund)
	for yard work.	(*for* + noun)

B Match each item on the left with one on the right that does a similar job.

1. burglar alarm
2. barbecue grill
3. washing machine
4. air conditioner

a. electric fan
b. vacuum cleaner
c. frying pan
d. smoke detector

C Pair work. Tell how the items in each pair above are similar and different.

> Both the burglar alarm and the smoke detector are used for protection.

D Group work. Take turns. Think of an object in your home. Describe it while your group's members guess.

> A: They're used for seeing things clearly.
> B: Is the answer *glasses*?
> A: No.
> C: Another clue, please.
> A: OK. They're used to see objects far away.
> D: I know! They're *binoculars*!

World Link

In Singapore, roughly 80% of 18-year-old males require glasses or contact lenses. Experts think this is due to longer hours spent watching TV, using computers, and studying.

Home improvement

> What is the most difficult or annoying household chore (indoors or outdoors)? Why do you think so?

 Pair work. Look at these three inventions. Guess what they are used for. Then read about them on page 154.

The Self-Propelled Shoe

The Electrolux Trilobite

The Bowlingual Translator

 Pair work. Design your own invention for the home. Draw a picture of it here and give it an imaginative name.

 Group work. Show the picture of your invention to another pair. Can they guess what it is?

Indoors and Outdoors

Lesson B | Public spaces

Public places and things

A Number each item in the picture below.

1. bus station
2. campus
3. newspaper stand
4. park
5. parking space
6. subway entrance
7. taxi stand
8. traffic light
9. parking meter

B How many times do you use these things or visit these places each week? Write numbers below.

bus station		newspaper stand		parking meter		subway entrance	
campus		park		parking space		taxi stand	

C Pair work. Take turns further explaining the answers you gave in B to your partner.

> I don't own a car, so I don't ever use parking spaces or parking meters.

> I go to the park every Sunday with my family.

ask & ANSWER

What are some other public places and things? How often do you visit them?

2 Listening

By car or by subway?

> Do you prefer to travel by car or to use public transportation? Why?

 A Ashley is asking José for help. Listen to the conversation and complete the sentence. (CD 1, Track 6)

Ashley wants to go to the _____.

 B Listen. Circle the answer to complete each sentence. (CD 1, Track 7)

1. Ashley wants to go by car / bus.
2. The driving directions are easy / hard.
3. The zoo is on Second / Church Avenue.

4. The subway entrance is near the park / newspaper stand.
5. You take the subway two / three stops.
6. The subway costs two / three dollars.

3 Reading

The father of American landscape architecture

> Where do you go to relax?

A Look at the photos on page 9. Then choose the answer to the definition.

A *landscape architect* _____.
a. designs parks and gardens   b. builds schools   c. gives tours

B Read the article. Then read these statements about Frederick Law Olmsted and his projects. Write *T* for true or *F* for false.

1. ____ Stanford University, Central Park, and Niagara Falls are in New York.
2. ____ Olmsted lived to be 90 years old.
3. ____ He and his partner won a contest.
4. ____ He fought against businesses.
5. ____ He wanted to make places beautiful.
6. ____ He would not like souvenir shops on Goat Island.

ask&
ANSWER
What's your favorite park? How can public parks be protected?

C Find words in the reading that are related in form to the ones below.

1. architect architecture
2. beauty _____
3. design _____

4. industry _____
5. nature _____
6. oppose _____

Creating Spaces

Jin Hee Park is a student at Stanford University in California. She studies hard. "Of course, I came here for the academics," she says. "But it doesn't hurt that the campus is so beautiful. I walk around sometimes just to relax."

Alejandro Vega, a banker in New York City jogs almost every evening after work in Central Park. "I never get bored. The park is so big. I can always find a different path with a new view."

Niagara Falls was on Ross Howard's list of places to visit in upstate New York. "The footpaths allow you to get a wonderful view. You can even feel the spray from the falls on your face."

What do these three places–Stanford University, Central Park, and Niagara Falls State Park–all have in common? They were all landscaped by Frederick Law Olmsted. Olmsted (1822-1903) has been called the "father of landscape architecture."

In the 1800s, more and more people were moving to the cities. Some community leaders became worried about the quality of life. They began a beautification campaign.

In 1857, a design contest was held for a new park in New York City. Olmsted and his partner, Calvert Vaux, won the contest. Central Park was the finished product—the first landscaped public park in the United States. Today, no trip to New York is complete without a visit to this beautiful park.

Later in his life, Olmsted designed landscapes for college campuses, including Stanford University. In the late 1860s, he joined the "Free Niagara" movement. Members of the movement wanted to preserve the beauty of Niagara Falls. Despite opposition and pressures from businesses to industrialize the area, Olmsted and others resisted. Olmsted designed footpaths to give visitors better views of the falls. In all his work, Olmsted preferred to preserve the natural beauty of an area.

Today, there are pressures again to develop Niagara. On Goat Island, an island in Niagara Falls State Park, there are now souvenir shops. There may be signs that say "No Littering," but there is still a lot of trash on the island. Most of the animals have disappeared. What would Frederick Law Olmsted say to all this?

Central Park

Niagara Falls

Frederick Law Olmsted

Stanford University

Expressing prohibition

 Match each sentence with the appropriate picture below.

1. _____ You aren't allowed to park here. Please use the parking lot.
2. _____ You're not supposed to touch the paintings. They're very old.
3. _____ Please step outside. You can't use your cell phone here.
4. _____ There's no smoking allowed here. Please wait until you exit the station.
5. _____ You mustn't drink and drive. You could have a serious car accident.
6. _____ After I hand out the tests, talking is forbidden.

B **Pair work. Look at the sentences in A. Underline the words that express prohibition. Then compare answers with a partner.**

C **Pair work. Think of two rules for each of the places below. Tell your partner.**

> *You can't carry a really large suitcase with you onto the airplane.*

| airplane park library museum |

Classroom rules

 Pair work. Make a list of "dos and don'ts" for the classroom. Write three rules students should follow in class and three rules about things that are prohibited.

B **Group work. Join another pair. Compare your lists. Then read them to the class.**

World Link

The Republic of Ireland became the first country in the world to ban smoking in all work places on March 29, 2004.

6 Communication

Which place would you protect?

What historical places have you visited? Which would you like to visit in the future?

A Read about these five places. Which one is the most interesting to you?

The Galapagos Islands (Ecuador)
Unique island "museum"

1,000 km from S. America, these 19 islands have animals and plants that developed without humans around.
Problem: Humans have introduced alien plants and animals to the islands.

Venice and its lagoon (Italy)
Famous cultural city

Founded in the 5th century, Venice lies on 118 islands and people travel by boats.
Problem: The water is rising every year and causing damage.

Angkor (Cambodia)
Magnificent ancient city

It contains ruins of more than 100 temples from the 9th to 15th centuries. It covers over 400 sq. km.
Problem: It is falling apart. The area is sometimes unsafe.

Timbuktu (Mali)
Ancient spiritual capital
It was a center for Islam in the 15th and 16th centuries. There are old buildings, including famous mosques.
Problem: Desert sands are covering up the city.

Lake Baikal (Russia)
World's oldest and deepest lake
It contains 20% of the world's unfrozen freshwater and a variety of marine and plant life.
Problem: Pollution is being poured into the lake.

B Group work. Imagine that you are on a special committee. You must choose one place to protect for the future. It can be one of the places above or a different one. Consider the questions below to help you with your decision. Report your decision to the class.

Is it important to history?
Is it rare or unique?
Is it very old?
Will many people visit it?

Is it beautiful?
Does it teach us about the earth?
Are the problems easy to fix?
Is it slowly disappearing?

Check out the World Link video.

Practice your English online at worldlink.heinle.com.

UNIT

2 Life Is All About Change

Lesson A | The times of your life

---

1 Vocabulary Link

The stages of life

A Use the words below to complete the information on the timeline.

1. childhood a
2. grown-up
3. infant b
4. middle-aged
5. teenager c
6. young

The Stages of Life

infancy a. _childhood_ adolescence   adulthood   old age

teen age

b. _infant_ / *child* *youth/* *adult/* *senior*
baby   *citizen*
            c. _teenager_   d. _grown-up_

e. _young_   f. _middle-aged_ **elderly**

0 - - - - - - - - - - - - - - - - - -- - - - -20 - - -40 - - -60 - -

---

B At what age do these events usually happen? Write the ages when most people first experience these events. Then write the ages when you first did them.

	People	Me		People	Me
1. say your first words	1	1	4. take a trip with friends	15	15
2. vote	18	18	5. go to a nightclub		—
3. get gray hair	45–50	40	6. buy a house/apartment	50–60	

C Pair work. Compare your answers with a partner. Ask questions about your partner's experiences.

ask&
ANSWER

At what age does a teenager become an adult? What do people do to celebrate or mark this event?

2 Listening

The terrible twos

> What do you think the phrase "the terrible twos" means?

 A **Listen to Ellie and Lee's conversation. Circle the correct answers.** (CD 1, Track 8)

1. Ellie is Brandon's ___.   **a.** sister   **b.** mother   **c.** aunt
2. Brandon ___ more now.   **a.** cries   **b.** laughs   **c.** talks

 B **Listen again. Circle *T* for true or *F* for false.** (CD 1, Track 9)

1. Brandon has a brother.   T   **F**   4. Brandon has changed.   **T**   F
2. Brandon had a birthday last week.   T   **F**   5. Lee has two infants.   T   **F**
3. Brandon was a good boy before.   **T**   F   6. Lee tells Ellie to be patient.   **T**   F

> **ask&**
> **ANSWER**
> What age do you think is the best age to be? Why?

3 Pronunciation

Emphasis patterns

 A **Listen to the following sentences. Notice how the <u>underlined</u> content words (nouns, verbs, adjectives, and adverbs) are stressed.** (CD 1, Track 10)

1. She's <u>spending</u> the <u>weekend</u> in the <u>city</u>.
2. Our <u>class</u> <u>begins</u> on <u>Monday</u>.
3. I'm going to <u>work</u> <u>hard</u> and <u>save</u> my <u>money</u>.
4. We're <u>buying</u> a <u>new</u> <u>car</u> <u>tomorrow</u>.
5. When I'm <u>forty</u>, I'll <u>live</u> in a <u>house</u> with a <u>big</u> <u>yard</u>.

B **Pair work. Take turns reading the sentences in A. Be sure to stress the content words.**

World Link

Humans have been born on all seven continents. The last of the seven was Antarctica—Emilio Marco Palma was born there in January 1978.

4 Speaking

I'm planning to rent a car.

A Listen to Peter and Sam's conversation. Underline Peter's plans. (CD 1, Track 11)

Sam: What are you doing?

Peter: I'm applying for a driver's license.

Sam: Congratulations! What are you planning to do when you get it?

Peter: Well, first, I'm going to take a trip.

Sam: Really? Where?

Peter: I'm going to visit my cousins in England.

Sam: Sounds like fun!

Peter: Yeah, and I'm planning to rent a car so I can get around.

Sam: That sounds great. Just be careful. They drive on the opposite side of the road there.

B Pair work. **Practice the conversation with a partner.**

Useful Expressions: Expressing intentions
I'm planning to rent a car. I'm going to visit my cousins. I plan/intend to get a driver's license. I'm thinking about buying a car.

5 Speaking Strategy

Expressing intentions

 A Pair work. **What do you think are these people's plans or intentions? Share your ideas with a partner. Use the Useful Expressions to help you.**

Penny

Diego

Tisha

 B Check (✓) the items you plan to do in the future. Add one more item to the list.

- ☐ take a big trip
- ☐ vote in an election
- ☐ apply for a credit card
- ☐ move
- ☐ make a big purchase
- ☐ _____

C Pair work. **Share your answers with a partner. Ask each other questions about the items you checked.**

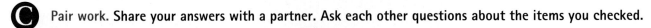

6 Language Link

Future forms

A Match the questions on the left with their answers on the right.

1. What do you plan to do this evening? *c*
2. How will school be different in the future? *d*
3. What are you doing on your vacation? *f*
4. When is your graduation? *b*
5. Do you need a tissue? *a*
6. Is that the telephone? *e*

a. Yes. Hurry! I'm going to sneeze.
b. The ceremony starts at 10:00 tomorrow.
c. I'm going to eat dinner and watch a video.
d. I think teenagers will have robots for teachers.
e. Yes, it is. I'll get it.
f. I'm traveling to Europe.

B Look at how future time is expressed in sentences a–f above. Then match each sentence a–f with 1–6 below.

12 sentences homework.

b 1. In which sentence is the present tense used for a scheduled event in the future?

d 2. In which sentence is *will* used for a general prediction?

e 3. In which sentence is *will* used for an action decided upon at the moment of speaking?

f 4. In which sentence is the present continuous used for future plans that have already been made?

a 5. In which sentence is *be going to* used for something about to happen?

c 6. In which sentence is *be going to* used for future plans or intentions?

C Complete the conversation below. Use a future form of the verbs in parentheses. In some cases there may be more than one answer possible.

A: I **(1. fly)** _am going to fly_ to Thailand tomorrow.
   or am flying
   My plane **(2. leave)** _leaves_ at 4:00.

B: Oh, really?

A: Yes. I **(3. visit)** _am going to visit_ my friend in Bangkok.
   There's only one problem. I don't have a ride to the airport.

B: Don't worry. I have a car. I **(4. take)** _will take_ you.

A: Thanks. Do you think I **(5. need)** _will need_ to pack
   my sweaters? *or going to need*

B: No. It **(6. be)** _will be_ warm there.

7 Communication

The Magic Answer Bag

> The Magic Answer Bag can tell your fortune. You ask it a question and then reach in and pull out your answer. Do you think some people or things can predict the future? Explain your answer.

 A Group work. Write each expression from the box below on a slip of paper and fold each paper. Each group puts the papers in a bag or hat.

Yes	No	Maybe
Absolutely!	No way!	It's possible.
For sure!	Not a chance!	Maybe.
Of course!	It's not going to happen!	Who knows?

B Work alone. What would you like to know about your future?
Think of four *yes/no* questions and write them down.

1. Will I get a good grade on my next exam? _____

2. _____

3. _____

4. _____

C Group work. You are now going to get answers to your questions. Ask the Magic Answer Bag your question. A member of your group should shake the bag, pull out an answer, and read it aloud.

Will I get a good grade on my next exam?

I'm sorry. The answer is "No way!"

D Group work. Discuss the Magic Answer Bag's answers.
Do you think they were accurate? Why or why not?

Life Is All About Change

Lesson B | Milestones   *important thing*

---

1 Vocabulary Link ⟷

Important events

A Match a word or expression in the box with a picture.

> 1. have a baby   3. get divorced   5. get promoted   7. move out
>
> 2. fall in love   4. get married   6. graduate   8. retire

4   A.   6   B.   7   C.   3   D.

8   E.   5   F.   1   G.   2   H.

B Some of life's events are happier than others. Rank the events above from 1–8
(1 = happiest, 8 = least happy). Compare your rankings with a partner.

ask & ANSWER

Which events above have you not yet experienced?
Are there any events you would like to avoid? Explain your answers.

A Mandy is working on a report for school. Her mother is helping her. Listen and complete the sentences below. (CD 1, Track 12)

refugees

Refugees are people who leave their

(1) _____ to escape

(2) __war_____ or other problems.

Worldwide, there are about

(3) __17,000,000___ refugees today.

Sadako Ogata

B Listen again. Check (✓) the events Ms. Ogata experienced in her life. (CD 1, Track 13)

1. [✓] worked at the United Nations
2. [ ] hosted a TV show
3. [✓] moved to the United States
4. [✓] graduated from college

5. [✓] got married
6. [ ] got divorced
7. [ ] wrote books
8. [✓] had children

ask&
ANSWER
Name a person you admire.
Why do you respect him or her?

3 Reading 📖

Life's stressors

> What are some words and images you associate with the word *stress*?

A In each pair below, which event do you think causes more stress? Check (✓) the boxes.

1. a. [ ] death of spouse
   b. [ ] personal injury

2. a. [ ] pregnancy
   b. [ ] retirement

3. a. [ ] divorce
   b. [ ] moving

B Read the article about life's stressors on page 19 and compare the information in the article with your answers in **A**.

World Link

According to a 2003 survey, high income consumers in Australia, Ja and the U.S. are the most stressed while those in Hong Kong and Br are the most laid back.

C Circle the correct answer.

Dr. Palmer thinks stressors are _____ events.

a. avoidable   c. major and minor

b. unhappy

COPING WITH LIFE'S STRESSORS

by Dr. Judy Palmer

Let's face it: Life is stressful. Stressful events in our lives are called "stressors." Some of them are minor, such as uncomfortable air conditioning or a loudly ringing telephone. Others are more serious, such as the death of a spouse. That event tops the list as life's most stressful event.

You might be surprised to learn about the top 20 life stressors. Getting a divorce, for example, is number 2 on the list. And not all stressors are unhappy events. Pregnancy is a happy time for most families. It may also cause stress. Pregnancy is right below retirement on the list of life's major stressors.

We can't avoid stress, but we can do something about it. Read below to learn about the healthy responses these people had to stress in their lives.

Tina Vega, 16

Last year was horrible! My family moved to another town. I had to change schools and say good-bye to all my friends. It was really tough. I felt so lonely in my new school. But then one day I decided to enjoy my life: I smiled at everyone and I joined the soccer club at school. Now I have new friends. I like my new school.

Frederick Cho, 42

Life is unpredictable. Three weeks ago I lost my job. I was upset for the first week. I couldn't do anything. Now I'm looking for a new job. It's not good to sit around the house. I exercise every day and I'm healthier than I've been in years.

Hazel Greene, 80

My husband and I got married in 1950. He died five years ago. For the first two years I was depressed. I missed him so much because we did everything together. But now I'm feeling better. I think it's important to stay active and positive. I read a lot and do volunteer work.

D Complete the chart below with information from the article. *sipline*

	What happened?	When did it happen?	How did the person feel at first?	What did the person do to relieve stress?
Tina Vega	moved to another town	last year	lonely	enjoy her life
Frederick Cho	lost his job	Three weeks ago	upset	exercise every day
Hazel Greene	her husband died	five years ago	depressed	read a lot / volunteer work

ask & ANSWER

Do you think life nowadays is more or less stressful than it was 50 years ago? Why? What is another example of a "happy stressor"? Have you experienced a happy stressor? Explain your answer.

disruptive things

4 Language Link

Modals of future possibility

 A Study the chart. Notice the modals of future possibility highlighted in blue.

Modals of future possibility	
Questions	Answers
Are you going to get promoted? Will you get promoted?	I may (not). I might (not). I could.
When are you getting married?	I may/might/could get married next summer.
The modal verbs highlighted in the chart indicate that something is possible in the future. They are all very similar in meaning when used this way.	

B Pair work. What will you do tomorrow? Check (✓) the box for yes (Y), no (N), or maybe (M). Ask your partner about his or her answers.

	Y	N	M			Y	N	M
1. get to class/work on time	☐	☐	✓		4. watch a lot of TV	☐	✓	☐
2. do English homework	✓	☐	☐		5. eat lunch alone	☐	☐	✓
3. talk on the telephone a lot	☐	✓	☐		6. bring an umbrella	☐	☐	✓

C Pair work. Ask your partner another question about his or her future.

Will you get to class on time?   *I may.*

5 Writing

My future

 A Look at the timeline. Then make a future timeline of your life. Put at least four events on it.

 B Write about the events on your timeline that *will* happen and the ones that *may* happen. Give details.

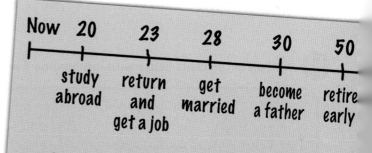

Now 20 23 28 30 50

study abroad — return and get a job — get married — become a father — retire early

Next year, I'm going to study abroad. I want to study business economics. It will help me in my career. When I'm 23, I may come home to look for a job.

 C Pair work. Share your writing with a partner. Ask and answer questions about the events on your timelines.

6 Communication

What will you do?

 A Complete this quiz about your future life.

have more than one pet

meet someone famous

travel somewhere fun or exciting

	I may/might	I will	I won't
1. get married more than once			✓
2. have at least two children	✓		
3. retire in 20 years			✓
4. take a dance class			✓
5. get promoted in my job	✓		
6. live alone			✓
7. travel somewhere fun or exciting		✓	
8. see or meet a famous person	✓		
9. learn to speak a foreign language		✓	
10. get a driver's license		✓	
11. have more than one pet			✓
12. buy a sports car	✓		

B Pair work. Interview your partner. Ask and answer questions about the chart above.

Will you have at least two children?

I think I will. I want to have a big family!

C Group work. Join another pair. Explain how you are similar to or different from each other.

 Check out the World Link video.　 **Practice your English online at** <u>worldlink.heinle.com.</u>

1 Vocabulary Link

Newsmakers

 A Look at the pictures. Then match each sentence with the job it describes.

1. A journalist writes stories for the newspaper. __A__
2. An international correspondent reports from abroad. _____
3. A cartoonist makes funny drawings for the newspaper. _____
4. A photographer takes pictures. _____
5. A copyeditor makes corrections before the newspaper is printed. _____
6. A publisher manages and publishes the newspaper. _____
7. A critic writes opinions about books, movies, and plays. _____
8. A news anchor reads the news from a TV studio. _____

B Answer these questions about the jobs in A. Then explain your answers to a partner.

Which job is the most . . . glamorous? boring? creative? dangerous?

ask&
ANSWER
Which of the jobs would you like to have? Why? Which ones would you not like to have? Why not?

2 Listening

A dangerous job

A Listen to the two conversations. Check (✓) Christiane's and Dan's job(s). (CD 1, Track 14)

Christiane Amanpour

☐ news anchor

☐ international correspondent

Dan Eldon

☐ journalist

☐ photographer

B Listen again. Write C if the statement refers to Christiane, D if it refers to Dan, and B if it refers to both. (CD 1, Track 15)

1. _____ a parent
2. _____ wrote a book
3. _____ reports from London

4. _____ born in London
5. _____ worked in dangerous places
6. _____ died on the job

3 Pronunciation

Hearing unclear vowels

A An unclear vowel sound is called a *schwa* (/ə/) in English. Listen to these sentences. Notice the schwa sounds in the underlined words. (CD 1, Track 16)

/ə/   /ə/ /ə/   /ə/   /ə/
1. Christiane is an international correspondent.

/ə/ /ə/   /ə/
2. Sid is the guy reporting on political problems.

/ə/   /ə/   /ə/ /ə/ /ə/
3. Mark is a famous fashion photographer.

B Pair work. Practice saying the sentences in A with unclear vowel sounds.

4 Speaking

Do you know him?

  A Peter is a reporter. He wants to interview the owner of a new restaurant and asks Peggy for help. Listen to their conversation. (CD 1, Track 17)

Peter: Hello. I'm Peter Daniels. I'm a reporter from the Center City News.

Peggy: It's nice to meet you, Mr. Daniels. My name is Peggy Sims.

Peter: Hi, Peggy. I'm looking for the owner of the Golden Pearl Restaurant. Do you know him?

Peggy: Yes. He's standing over there.

Peter: That tall man in the sweater?

Peggy: No, that's an employee. The owner is the man wearing the suit.

Peter: Oh, I see him. Thanks a lot.

 B Pair work. **Practice the conversation with a partner.**

5 Speaking Strategy

Asking about identity

 A Class activity. **Read and follow the directions.**

Pat Rich is a multi-millionaire who has been hiding for many years and using a false name. *The Daily News* has discovered that Pat is in your classroom! Who is he or she?

Group A: You are newspaper reporters for *The Daily News*. Gather on one side of the room. Don't listen to Group B's discussion!

Group B: Choose one person to be Pat Rich. Remember to whisper! You don't want the students in Group A to hear!

 B Class activity. **Now follow these directions.**

Group A: Now walk around the room and ask about the identity of Pat Rich. When you know who Pat is, sit down. Try not to be the last person standing!

Group B: Only give out one detail per person. Don't use *he* or *she* in your clues!

> **Useful Expressions:**
> Asking about identity
>
> Who is Pat Rich?
> Do you know Pat Rich?
> Is that Pat Rich?
> Do you know who Pat Rich is?
> Can you tell me who Pat Rich is?

Who is Pat Rich?

Pat is wearing white socks.

6 Language Link

Describing people with prepositional and participial phrases

 A Study the chart. Notice the prepositional and participial phrases highlighted in blue.

Questions	Answers
Do you know who the publisher is?	He's the man sitting at the desk. [participial phrase]
Can you tell me who the publisher is?	He's the guy with glasses. [prepositional phrase]
Who is the editor?	He's the person wearing a tie. [participial phrase]
Do you know Ms. Amanpour?	Yes. She's the one on TV. [prepositional phrase]
Is that Ms. Amanpour?	No. Ms. Amanpour is the woman interviewing the man. [participial phrase]

 B Pair work. Role play. **Read and follow these instructions. Then switch roles and do the activity again.**

Student A: You are a newspaper reporter reporting on a bank robbery. Use participial or prepositional phrases to ask the police chief about the identity of the four suspects below. Then ask the chief's opinion about who the bank robber is.

Student B: You are the police chief. Use your imagination to answer the reporter's questions about each suspect's identity.

Who is the woman with the cell phone?

The one wearing the purple jacket? That's Mary Moffit. I found her near the bank with a briefcase full of money!

 C Pair work. A new student has transferred into your school. Imagine that you are in the teacher's room at school. Take turns describing the teachers to the new student.

Mr. Marshall is the one with a mustache. He teaches English.

Jobs in journalism

 A Group work. **Circle the choices that best describe you. Share your answers.**

1. I prefer speaking / writing in English.
2. I want my future job to be exciting / predictable.
3. I don't mind working alone / with a lot of people.
4. I am good / not good at meeting deadlines.
5. People would probably say my personality is outgoing / shy.
6. I like to have a quiet / busy schedule.
7. I like to spend time indoors / outdoors.
8. I prefer to work and travel near my home / all over the place.
9. I prefer to be happy / well-paid in my job.
10. I do well on creative / detail-oriented jobs.

 B Group work. **Read about these jobs. Based on your answers in A, decide the best person for each job.**

Web-based movie critic
Work alone at home. Watch movies and write about them for our website. Submit work every Thursday. The salary isn't high, but you get to see all the latest movies for free!

Writer: *Travel for Pennies* **magazine**
Travel with a photographer and write articles about traveling cheaply. You'll have to live on a tight budget, but you can travel the world!

Editorial assistant
Work with a large staff in a newsroom. Research news stories, gather photos, and check facts. Good salary and benefits in a busy office atmosphere.

International correspondent: *Hot Spots* **TV show**
Our correspondents file reports from the most exciting, dangerous places in the world. No two days are the same! You'll meet interesting people and interview them. Competitive salary.

Newspapers and the News

1 Vocabulary Link

My favorite newspaper

A Use the words below to complete each person's opinion.

a. comics	c. headlines	e. ~~published~~	g. sections	i. ~~subscribe~~
b. daily	d. horoscope	f. scan	h. sensational	j. weather forecast

Every morning, the newspaper is delivered to my house. I **(1)** _subscribe_. It's cheaper than buying it at the newsstand every day. There are so many different **(2)** _____ : sports and business, for example. I only have a few minutes in the morning. The first thing I do is quickly **(3)** _____ the **(4)** _____ on the front page. Then I decide what to read. It's embarrassing, but I like to read the **(5)** _____ stories the best. I just love the drama!

My town's newspaper is **(6)** _published_ **(7)** _____, but I only read it on Sundays. That's the day they have a full page of **(8)** _____ —I love cartoons! They make me smile. There's also the **(9)** _____ page. On that page I can look up my star sign and read about my future. On Thursdays in the summer, I check the **(10)** _____. I like to go to the beach on the weekend.

B Pair work. Answer these questions about newspapers and the news. Compare your answers with a partner.

1. My favorite newspaper or magazine is published ___.
   a. daily   b. weekly   c. monthly

2. I always read the ___ first.
   a. headlines   c. entertainment news
   b. sports section   d. other: _____

3. I subscribe to ___ newspapers and magazines.
   a. 0   b. 1   c. 2   d. more than 2

4. I read/listen to the weather forecast ___.
   a. in the newspaper   c. on TV
   b. on the Internet   d. other: _____

ask& ANSWER

What do you like most about your favorite newspaper or magazine?
How do you usually get your news?

2 Listening 🎧

Do you like *The Daily News?*

> Think of two popular newspapers. How are they similar? How are they different?

🔊 **A** **Listen. Maria and Joe are talking about** *The Daily News.* **Circle the correct words.** (CD 1, Track 18)

1. Maria likes / dislikes *The Daily News.*   2. Joe likes / dislikes *The Daily News.*

🔊 **B** **Listen again. What are Maria and Joe's opinions about** *The Daily News?* **Check (✓) the boxes.**
(CD 1, Track 19)

1. What does Maria like about it?

☐ the comics page   ☐ the horoscope

☐ the news coverage   ☐ the price

2. What does Joe dislike about it?

☐ the weather forecast   ☐ the news coverage

☐ the price   ☐ the headlines

3 Reading 📖

Nutty news

A **Skim the two news articles on page 29. Then write a headline for each one. Compare your headlines with those of a partner.**

First story: _____   Second story: _____

B **Read the two news articles. Underline at least six examples of the present perfect.**

C **Read the news articles again. Find the words that match the meanings below.**

Article 1
1. brought into your family _____
2. look into _____
3. injured and unable to react _____
4. an animal doctor _____

Article 2
1. the end point of your travels _____
2. having a document saying you are qualified to do something _____
3. the areas of a city that are farthest away from the center _____
4. can't be damaged by water _____

D **On a separate piece of paper, write a brief summary of each article. Use the words you found in C.**

ask&
ANSWER
What's the most unusual news article you have ever heard or read? What exactly happened?

①

NUTTY NEWS

Kangaroo To The Rescue!

Lulu is a kangaroo. For 10 years she has lived with the Richards family. Lulu was adopted by the family after they found her next to her dead mother.

Mr. Ken Richards is a farmer. He was working on his farm when a heavy tree branch suddenly fell on top of him.

Lulu stood next to Mr. Richards' body. She started barking and didn't leave Mr. Richards' side.

"I've never heard Lulu bark like that—she sounded like a dog. She barked and barked and she didn't stop," said Celeste, Mr. Richards' daughter.

After 15 minutes, the Richards family went to investigate. They found Ken on the ground and he was unconscious.

"Lulu is a hero," said Celeste. "She saved my father."

Mr. Middleton, an expert veterinarian, said that Lulu's story is rare. "I have never seen a kangaroo act like that. Maybe Lulu helped Ken Richards because the Richards family is the only family she has ever known."

Lulu has always followed Ken around the farm. She's a loyal, friendly, and very intelligent kangaroo. After Ken leaves the hospital, he is planning to go everywhere with Lulu.

②

NUTTY NEWS

An Underwater Post Office?

Approximately 175,000 people live in the Republic of Vanuatu, an island chain east of Australia. It is a popular tourist destination because there's a lot to do there: you can visit waterfalls, go horseback riding, take an aerial tour, or visit a traditional Ni-Vanuatu village. Vanuatu is most famous for its scuba diving and snorkeling.

In an effort to draw attention to these popular water sports, Vanuatu has created a world's "first": the government has opened an underwater post office. You have to be a certified scuba diver to work there. The office is three meters below the surface in an area on the outskirts of Port Vila, the capital city.

So far, the post office has hired four workers. They will work in a room surrounded by the beauty of Vanuatu's underwater world. Customers will buy waterproof postcards on land and then dive down to the post office to receive a special waterproof stamp.

4 Language Link

Review of the present perfect

> **Be careful!**
> For events at a specific time (period) in the past, use the simple past.
> *I lived in Tokyo from 1998–1999.*
> *I bought that magazine yesterday.*

A Study the chart.

Use the present perfect for actions that began in the past and continue in the present.
I'm a reporter at *The Daily Sun News*. I've worked here for three years.
You can also use the present perfect to talk about actions that happened in the past, when the time they happened isn't important.
Have you ever read this magazine?
Use the present perfect with *just* for an action that has been completed recently.
I've just finished with the newspaper. You can borrow it now.

B Complete this news story with the verbs in parentheses. Use the present perfect or the simple past.

Bruno Hoffman lives near Toft Park. Every morning for the past 10 years, he (**1.** take) _____ a walk in the park.

Yesterday a strange thing (**2.** happen) _____. In the park, a squirrel (**3.** jump) _____ onto his shoulder. It wouldn't leave. When Bruno (**4.** brush) _____ it off, it (**5.** jump) _____ up again.

At that point, Bruno (**6.** call) _____ the police. "A friendly squirrel (**7.** attack) _____ just _____ me," he said.

"I (**8.** hear) _____ never _____ of such a thing," admitted the police officer who answered the call. He (**9.** advise) _____ Bruno to call an animal shelter for help.

Since the squirrel incident, Bruno (**10.** stop) _____ walking in Toft Park. He now walks on an indoor track.

5 Writing

An unusual news story

A Read this unusual news story. Then write your own unusual news story.

B Pair work. Exchange stories with a partner. Write a headline for your partner's story.

> **DOGGIE DRIVER**
> Traffic in Sharpville came to a sto
> yesterday afternoon when a car, dri
> a big dog, rolled through town.
> Police are still investigating, but su
> that students from the local universi
> may be behind the trick . . .

6 Communication

Conducting an interview

You've learned about comics and the horoscope section. What are some other sections of a newspaper?

A Where would you find these newspaper stories? Match each story on the left with the newspaper section it would appear in on the right.

1. _____ the mayor's divorce
2. _____ an interview with a famous soccer player
3. _____ a review of the newest movies
4. _____ stock market predictions
5. _____ an article about getting a college degree online

a. sports section
b. gossip column
c. business section
d. technology
e. arts and entertainment

B Choose a famous person to role-play. Write the name. What field does the person work in? Check (✓) the box.

Name of person: _____

☐ sports   ☐ business   ☐ arts and entertainment   ☐ other: _____

C Pair work. Role play. Ask your partner the name of the person he or she has chosen to role-play. Write six questions you would like to ask that person.

1. _____ ?
2. _____ ?
3. _____ ?
4. _____ ?
5. _____ ?
6. _____ ?

D Pair work. Role play. Imagine that you are a newspaper reporter. Interview your partner. Then switch roles.

 Check out the World Link video.

 Practice your English online at <u>worldlink.heinle.com.</u>

1 Storyboard

A Fran is returning a broken smoke detector. Look at the pictures and complete the conversations. More than one answer is possible for each blank.

B Group work. Practice the conversation in groups of three. Then change roles and practice again.

2 See it and say it

A Look at the picture below. Answer the questions.

- • Where are these people?
- • What are they doing? Why are they doing it?

B Describe what each person is planning to do in the future. Say as much as you can about each person's plans.

> Daisuke is thinking about buying a houseboat. He wants to live on the water. He'll probably become an artist.

C Pair work. Tell your partner what you plan to do in the future. Where do you plan to live? What kind of work do you plan to do?

3 I don't need it.

 A Match the words in the boxes to make compound words that name people or things.

1. _____ air   a. anchor
2. _____ barbecue   b. citizen
3. _____ driver's   c. conditioner
4. _____ movie   d. critic
5. _____ news   e. forecaster
6. _____ ranch   f. grill
7. _____ senior   g. house
8. _____ weather   h. license

 B Write the compound words you matched in A in the chart below.

People	Things
1.	1.
2.	2.
3.	3.
4.	4.

C Pair work. Talk about the people and things in B.
- Tell your partner which things you don't have or need.
- Tell your partner which people you'd like to be.

I'd like to be a movie critic because I could see movies for free!

4 Listening: An old family photo

  A Listen as John and Amy talk about a photo. Use the names in the box to label the people in the picture. (CD 1, Track 20)

~~John~~	Joseph
Olivia	Randy
Tina	Tom

B Listen again. Answer the questions below. (CD 1, Track 21)

1. Who put up the picture?   ☐ Olivia   ☐ Joseph   ☐ Tom

2. Who has an aunt named Olivia?   ☐ Tina   ☐ John   ☐ Amy

3. Who is married now?   ☐ Joseph   ☐ Tina   ☐ Randy

4. Who is in high school now?   ☐ Randy   ☐ Tina   ☐ Olivia

C Class activity. Do you have a picture of family members in your wallet or bag? Show your picture to the class and talk about it.

> The person standing in front of me is my sister. Her name is . . .

5 Swimming pool rules

A Pair work. Look at the picture. Take turns telling the rules at the swimming pool.

> One of the rules is "No dogs allowed."

B Class activity. Make up a list of rules for your classroom and share them with the class.

6 Using computers

A Complete the chart with the various uses of computers.

Computers can be used to . . .	Computers can be used for . . .
1. download music	typing reports for school
2.	
3.	

B Imagine that you received a brand new computer. How would you use it?

> I'd use my computer to download music and send e-mail messages to friends.

1 Vocabulary Link

Describing men and women

A Look at the pictures and read about these famous people.

David Beckham is not only an athletic soccer player. He's handsome, too.

Nick Lachey and Jessica Simpson are pop singers. They make an attractive couple, don't you think?

You probably imagi_ that Madonna is tall. Actually, she's petite! She's also ver_ athletic: she rides he_ bike and does yoga.

Stone Cold Steve Austin is a big, mean wrestler. He's well built and he's bald.

Lucy Liu is a pretty actress. She is going to a big event and looks very elegant i_ her designer gown.

B Now write the name of another famous person beside each adjective. Share your answers with the class.

1. well built _____
2. athletic _____
3. handsome _____
4. attractive _____

5. petite _____
6. bald _____
7. pretty _____
8. elegant _____

ask**&**
ANSWER

What makes a man handsome? What makes a woman pretty?

2 Listening

On the red carpet

 A Listen to these interviews with famous people attending an awards ceremony. Match the names to their occupations. (CD 1, Track 22)

1. _____ Joan Riverton   a. TV actress
2. _____ Debra Danvers   b. soccer star
3. _____ Marla Kelly   c. announcer
4. _____ Brad Litz   d. movie actress
5. _____ Yasmin   e. director

 B What does Joan Riverton say to each person directly? Listen again and complete the sentences. (CD 1, Track 23)

1. Debra: "You look so _____!"
2. Marla: "You're as _____ as a picture!"
3. Brad: "Don't you look _____ in that suit!"
4. Yasmin: "You're always so _____!"

 C Listen again and match the items with the words used to describe them. (CD 1, Track 24)

1. _____ dress   a. terrible
2. _____ earrings   b. nightmare
3. _____ movie   c. cheap
4. _____ suit   d. disaster

3 Pronunciation

Listing items in a series

 A Listen to the following sentences. Notice how the final item in a series has a falling intonation. (CD 1, Track 25)

1. Joan interviewed Debra, Marla, Brad, and Yasmin.
2. The winner will receive a diamond ring, a new sports car, and $50,000.
3. We need to get some juice, soda, and coffee.

 B Work with a partner. Practice saying the sentences. Use falling intonation on the final item in each sentence.

 C Complete the chart below. Share your answers with a partner using correct intonation.

My luckiest numbers	
My hardest subjects in school	
Famous people I want to meet	

My luckiest numbers are 7, 11, and 21.

4 Speaking

I'm getting a tattoo!

A Listen to Chris and Tyler's conversation. Why doesn't Tyler like tattoos? Underline his reasons. (CD 1, Track 26)

Chris: Guess what? I'm getting a tattoo.

Tyler: Are you serious? Why?

Chris: Oh, I've always wanted one. I've already waited for two years. Now I'm ready!

Tyler: I don't think you should get one.

Chris: Why not?

Tyler: Well, for one thing, it's going to hurt.

Chris: I know. That's what everyone says.

Tyler: For another, tattoos aren't easy to remove. What happens if you change your mind?

Chris: You sound like my mom. She's not very happy about my decision either.

B Pair work. Practice the conversation with a partner.

5 Speaking Strategy

Giving more than one reason

> **Useful Expressions:**
> Giving more than one reason
>
> For one thing . . . For another . . .
>
> In the first place . . . In the second . . .
>
> First of all . . . Second of all . . .

A Look at the pictures. Who usually does these things? Check M for men only, W for women only, or B for both.

get a tattoo

☐ M ☐ W ☐ B

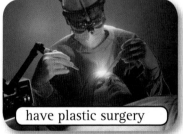

have plastic surgery

☐ M ☐ W ☐ B

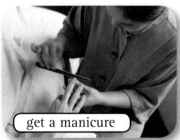

get a manicure

☐ M ☐ W ☐ B

wear makeup

☐ M ☐ W ☐ B

get your ears pierced

☐ M ☐ W ☐ B

B Pair work. Compare your responses. Give reasons why men and women should or shouldn't do the things in A.

I don't think men should wear makeup.

Why not?

The present perfect with *already, just, never, still,* **and** *yet*

A On June 16, Jin asked Mi-ran to marry him. She said yes. Read Mi-ran's diary entries for June 17 and September 20. Study the sentences.

> Date June 17
> Jin and I have **just** gotten engaged. I have **already** told my best friend the good news. I haven't told my parents **yet**. But I will very soon.

> Date September 20
> The wedding plans are moving forward. Jin and I have sent the invitations **already**. I'm nervous. I **still** haven't bought my wedding dress.

B Complete the statements with the words in bold in A.

1. You can use _____ and _____ with affirmative verbs in the present perfect.
2. You can use _____ and _____ with negative verbs in the present perfect.
3. _____ can be placed in the middle of the sentence or at the end of the sentence.

C Read the two conversations. Add the adverb in parentheses to the sentences that precede them. Then practice the conversations with a partner.

February 2

Bob: Hey, Colin. What's wrong?
Colin: It's Sally. She hasn't called. (still) I gave her my phone number two days ago.
Bob: Be patient! You've met her. (just)

One month later

Bob: Has Sally called? (yet)
Colin: Yes. We've gone on six dates. (already)
Bob: That's great!
Colin: Yeah. And I've asked her to meet my parents! (already)

D Circle the sentence that best follows the first sentence.

1. He's never exercised.
   a. He's really well built.
   b. He's out of shape.

2. I've just met Paula.
   a. She's nice.
   b. She's an old friend.

3. I've already gotten a tattoo.
   a. Should I do it?
   b. I really like it!

4. I haven't finished yet.
   a. I'd better hurry.
   b. I did a good job!

5. We still haven't met Sammy.
   a. Will he be at the party?
   b. He's a friendly guy!

6. I haven't seen the doctor yet.
   a. I saw him yesterday.
   b. I'm seeing him later.

7 Communication

Act like a man

 A Read these statements. Check (✓) if you *agree, disagree,* **or are** *not sure.*

Statements about men and women	agree	disagree	not sure
1. Wives should always listen to their husbands.			
2. Men are stronger than women.			
3. A woman should never ask a man on a date.			
4. Men are hotheaded.			
5. Women are good listeners.			
6. Men worry about their appearance more than women.			
7. Women can't accept criticism well.			
8. Men are too competitive.			
9. Athletic women are not attractive to men.			
10. Emotional men are too weak.			

B Group work. Work with three other students. Compare and explain your answers from A. If one or more group members disagreed or was not sure, check (✓) the box of that item below.

1. ☐   6. ☐

2. ☐   7. ☐

3. ☐   8. ☐

4. ☐   9. ☐

5. ☐   10. ☐

It says that "Men are stronger than women."

Men have stronger bodies, but women can be stronger in other ways. I checked "not sure."

C Group work. As a group, work on each statement you checked in B. Rewrite the statement so that *everyone* agrees with it.

D Group work. Present your group's statements to the class.

World Link

Junko Tabei of Japan was the first woman to climb Mt. Everest when she reached the summit on May 16, 1975.

ask & ANSWER

Do you think men and women have changed in the last 20 years? If so, how have they changed? If not, why haven't they changed?

Men and Women

Lesson B | Dating

1 Vocabulary Link

Friends first

A Read Ethan's personal ad. Then match each word with its definition below.

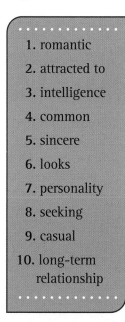

1. romantic
2. attracted to
3. intelligence
4. common
5. sincere
6. looks
7. personality
8. seeking
9. casual
10. long-term relationship

Address: http://www.wlfriends.net   › GO

★ **Let's Be Friends First** ★

- Romantic guy looking for partner for long walks at sunset and candlelit dinners.
- Are you attracted to intelligence? Do you like smart guys? I'm a software engineer and I like to solve puzzles.
- For relaxation, I enjoy swimming, tennis, and going to the movies. I hope that we can share common interests.
- Honesty is important to me, so I hope you'll be sincere in your response.
- Good looks are important, too, but beauty isn't everything. You should also have a good personality.
- Seeking a casual dating situation. If it leads to a long-term relationship, that's great!
- Looking forward to hearing from you.   ✉ 2622

a. ____ character
b. ____ real or true
c. ____ interested in (romantically)
d. ____ looking for
e. ____ appearance
f. ____ informal
g. ____ related to love and romance
h. ____ the ability to understand a lot of things
i. ____ the same or identical
j. ____ serious dating

B What qualities are important to you when you are dating? Rank the items from 1 to 3 within each group. (1 = most important, 3 = least important). Compare your answers with a partner's.

A	B	C
___ intelligence	___ romantic person	___ long-term relationship
___ looks	___ sincere person	___ casual dating
___ personality	___ common interests	___ wait and see

ANSWER

Why do you think some people use personal ads? Are personal ads a good way to meet someone?

2 Listening

Just talk to him!

 A Listen to Kylie and Alex's conversation. Then complete each sentence with a word from the box. (CD 1, Track 27)

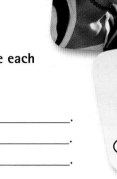

> classmates
>
> friends
>
> teammates

1. Kylie and Alex are _____.
2. Kylie and Gabe are _____.
3. Alex and Gabe are _____.

 B Listen again. Circle *T* for true, *F* for false, or *NM* for not mentioned. (CD 1, Track 28)

1. Kylie likes Gabe.	T	F	NM
2. Kylie and Gabe are in the same science class.	T	F	NM
3. Gabe likes Kylie.	T	F	NM
4. Alex thinks Gabe is nice.	T	F	NM
5. Kylie approaches Gabe.	T	F	NM

ask**&**
ANSWER

Should girls approach boys?
Why or why not?

3 Reading

Dating styles

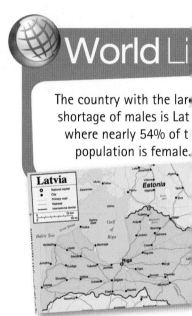

World Li

The country with the lar shortage of males is Lat where nearly 54% of t population is female.

> How do you usually meet people?

A Scan the article on page 43. Check (✓) the different dating styles that are mentioned.

- [ ] a blind date
- [ ] going out with friends
- [ ] a personal introduction
- [ ] a matchmaking party
- [ ] Internet dating
- [ ] speed dating

B Read the article on page 43. Only one statement below is true for each person. For the false one, change it to make it true.

1. Deepak matched with two women.
2. Deepak prefers tradition.
3. Nina grew up in Mexico City.
4. Nina relaxes more easily with friends.
5. Kaleo loves water sports.
6. Kaleo has already tried Internet dating.
7. Fumiko didn't enjoy the party.
8. Fumiko has practical ideas about dating.

ask**&**
ANSWER

Would you try any of the dating methods mentioned in the reading? Why or why not?

DATING AROUND THE WORLD

Do you want to go on a date? Are you still single?
So are these people! We asked them two questions:

Q1: How did you recently try to meet someone?

Q2: How would you like to meet someone?

After you read their responses, you may realize something:
Meeting someone special can be a challenge anywhere!

Deepak, London

Q1: I went to a "speed dating" event in London. There is a long table. Boys sit on one side and girls sit on the other. You talk to the person sitting across from you. After three minutes a bell rings, and you move on to the next person. You check off the names of the people you like. It was fun, but three minutes is too short! I didn't make any matches!

Q2: I'd like to have someone introduce me to a nice girl. I don't like casual dating. Maybe I'm too traditional, but that's how I am.

Nina, Mexico City

Q1: I grew up in a small town before I moved to the big city. Back home, there was a guy I was attracted to, but I never talked to him. Recently, I've tried to meet men here, but I'm still too shy!

Q2: It's more relaxing to go out in a big group. I want to meet someone when I'm out with a group of friends. That feels more natural and not so stressful.

Kaleo, Honolulu

Q1: I met a woman at work. I asked her out, but it caused problems. I need to find a new place for meeting women.

Q2: Of course, looks are important, but I want to meet someone with common interests. I love waterskiing and surfing. My friend says that Internet dating is fun. You can read all about the other person before you contact her. That might work for me.

umiko, Osaka

Q1: I went to a kind of "matchmaking party." There are the same number of boys and girls at the party. It's not very romantic. And when I attended, the drinks were very expensive!

Q2: I'd like to meet someone by myself in a romantic way. Imagine this: there is a huge rainstorm. A handsome stranger shares his umbrella with you. You and he fall in love. I know it sounds crazy, but that's my fantasy.

A Look at the pictures and read the story about Gus and Erin. Underline the phrasal verbs (verbs made up of more than one word) under the pictures.

1. Gus liked Erin. One day he <u>asked</u> her <u>out</u> on a date.

2. Erin was shy. At first she turned Gus down.

3. Gus asked Erin again and she said yes. She agreed to go out with him.

4. Gus and Erin enjoyed spending time together. They got along well.

5. Unfortunately, Gus cheated on Erin. She saw him with another girl.

6. Erin was very upset. She broke up with Gus.

7. Erin and Gus don't date anymore, but sometimes they run into each other.

8. Erin and Gus stopped dating three months ago, but Gus still can't get over her.

B Match each underlined phrasal verb above with its meaning.

a. _____ liked each other   e. _____ stop thinking about; recover
b. _____ invited   f. _____ spend time with; date
c. _____ meet unexpectedly   g. _____ stopped dating
d. _____ refused   h. _____ was unfaithful to

5 Writing

A personal ad

A Write your own personal ad. Use the questions below to help you.

What do you do?

What do you do in your free time?

How would you describe your personality?

What are you looking for in another person?

B Pair work. Exchange papers with a partner. Make suggestions that you think will improve your partner's ad.

Do you like to travel?
Busy student seeks travel partner during summer vacation. Looking for curious people. Let's explore the world together! I'm fun-loving and easy to get along with. You should be friendly and athletic.

A Complete this dating survey.

Dating Survey

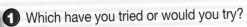

1 Which have you tried or would you try?

a. Internet dating
b. personal ads
c. going on a double date
d. going on a blind date
e. _____

2 The best way to attract someone is to

a. be friendly.
b. compliment them.
c. act shy.
d. not do anything special.
e. _____

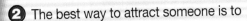

3 What *first* attracts you to a person?

a. looks
b. personality
c. intelligence
d. having common interests
e. _____

4 How do you know you really like someone?

a. My heart beats faster around him or her.
b. I can't stop thinking about him or her.
c. I have a dream about him or her.
d. I can relax around him or her.
e. _____

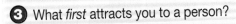

5 Your boyfriend or girlfriend has cheated on you. What do you do?

a. end the relationship
b. ignore it
c. talk to him or her
d. wait for him or her to talk to you
e. _____

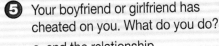

6 What should you definitely do on a first date?

a. bring a gift
b. talk a lot
c. offer to split the bill
d. wear something fancy
e. _____

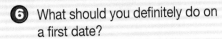

7 In a difficult situation, how would you break up with someone?

a. over the telephone
b. by e-mail or text message
c. face-to-face
d. by ignoring the person
e. _____

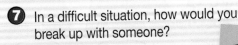

8 Which is the *worst* dating situation?

a. Your date shows up an hour late.
b. Your date complains about his or her last date.
c. Your date doesn't have enough money.
d. Your date doesn't dress attractively.
e. _____

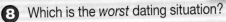

B Pair work. Compare your answers with a partner. Which answers were different? Explain your answers.

 Check out the World Link video.

 Practice your English online at <u>worldlink.heinle.com.</u>

5 Being Different

Lesson A | How to behave

1 Vocabulary Link

Table manners

 A This family is about to have a holiday dinner. Look at the picture and read the sentences.

1. It's typical to seat the head of the household at the head of the table.
2. It's unusual not to put a baby in a special chair.
3. It's disrespectful to interrupt someone who is talking.
4. Chewing gum loudly is offensive.
5. It's impolite to arrive late.
6. Bringing a small gift is appropriate.

B Circle the best answer to complete each definition.

1. When you see *offensive* behavior, you feel happy / upset.
2. *Unusual* behavior is surprising / not surprising because it's not normal.
3. *Typical* behavior is behavior that happens most of the time / rarely.
4. An *impolite* person is a kind / rude person.
5. An *appropriate* action is the correct / incorrect thing to do.
6. A *disrespectful* person worries / doesn't care about offending people.

 C Complete the chart of positive and negative words. Use the words in the box.

atypical
usual
inappropriate
inoffensive
polite
respectful

Positive words	Negative words
appropriate	_in___
_____	disrespectful
_____	impolite
_____	offensive
typical	_____
	unusual

> Have you ever been on a guided tour? What place or places did you visit on the tour?

A Listen to this guide talking about a guided tour of Colorado Cave. What is *not* allowed inside the cave? Check the boxes. (CD 1, Track 29)

| ☐ flashlights | ☑ gum | ☑ touching rocks |
| ☑ food | ☑ taking photos | ☐ wheelchairs |

B Listen again. Match the items on the left with the words that describe them on the right. (CD 1, Track 30)

Colorado Cave

1. _b_ tour   a. fine
2. _d_ rock formations   b. typical
3. _a_ wheelchair   c. interesting
4. _e_ path   d. unusual
5. _c_ gift shop   e. not steep

3 Pronunciation

Linking consonant to consonant

A A consonant sound at the end of a word links to the same consonant sound at the beginning of the next word. The two consonants are not pronounced separately. Listen to these sentences. (CD 1, Track 31)

1. I left two dollars for a tip.
2. He had doughnuts for breakfast.
3. She'll learn to be respectful.
4. Use a clean napkin.
5. This is delicious soup.
6. Keep practicing polite behavior.

B Pair work. Practice saying the sentences in A. Be sure to link the consonant sounds.

World Link

Tipping is common in many countries around the world, including the U.S., Egypt, Mexico, Italy, and Thailand.

4 Speaking

I'll explain everything.

A Listen to Inez and Ahmed's conversation at the International Club dinner. What does Inez think of Turkish food? (CD 1, Track 32)

Ahmed: Hi, Inez! Welcome! You're the first guest to arrive.

Inez: Hi, Ahmed.

Ahmed: I hope you're hungry. I made a lot of food.

Inez: Wow! How long did it take?

Ahmed: A few hours. But don't worry. Cooking Turkish food is fun.

Inez: It looks delicious. Can I sit anywhere?

Ahmed: Sure, go ahead. Make yourself comfortable.

Inez: I've never had Turkish food. I don't know what to eat first.

Ahmed: Don't worry. I'll explain everything. Try some of this cabbage dolma.

Inez: Mmmm. That's good!

B Pair work. Practice the conversation with a partner.

5 Speaking Strategy

Asking about rules

A Read about these two situations. Then look at the rules for each situation.

"I'm going to visit a mosque for the first time in my life."

"I've been invited to a formal Japanese dinner."

Rules	Yes	No
wear shoes inside		✓
wear shorts		✓
wear a scarf (women)	✓	
sit with my sister (men)		✓

Rules	Yes	No
help myself to a drink		✓
make special food requests		✓
ask to use a knife and fork	✓	
leave a tip		✓

B Pair work. Role play. Role-play one of the situations above with a partner. One person asks about the rules. The other person explains them.

Is it OK to wear shoes inside the mosque?　　*No. You have to remove them.*

C Pair work. Role play. Switch roles and role-play the other situation.

> **Useful Expressions:**
> Asking about rules
>
> Can I . . . ?
> May I . . . ?
> Is it all right/OK to . . . ?
> Is it all right/OK if I . . . ?

It + *be* + adjective + infinitive; gerund as subject

 A Read about these six customs. How are these customs similar to or different from customs in your own country?

1. **Eating**
   Having bread with your meal is typical in France.

2. **Conversation**
   It's important to maintain eye contact when speaking to someone in Chile.

3. **Physical affection**
   Showing physical affection in public is inappropriate in Myanmar.

4. **Greeting people**
   It's customary to shake hands when you meet someone in Kenya.

5. **Time**
   It's important to be on time for appointments in Switzerland.

6. **Tipping**
   Tipping taxi drivers is unnecessary in Finland.

 B Read the information in the box. Then rewrite each custom from A in a different way.

It + *be* + adjective + infinitive	Gerund as subject
It's **impolite to talk** with food in your mouth.	**Talking** with food in your mouth is **impolite**.
These two structures express the same meaning.	

1. It's typical to have bread with your meal in France.
2. Maintaining eye contact when speaking to someone in Japan is important.
3. It is inappropriate to show physical affection in public in Japan. ✓
4. Shaking hands when you meet someone in Japan is atypical.
5. _____
6. _____

 C Pair work. Imagine that you and your partner are writing a guidebook about your country or a country you know. On a separate piece of paper, write one important rule that a visitor would want to know about each item in the box.

eating	conversation	physical affection
greetings	time	tipping

A *culture capsule* is a container of items from your culture. The container can be as big as you want. This container is buried in the earth for people to find many years in the future. The items in the capsule can show people in the future something about your culture.

 Pair work. With a partner, imagine that you are going to make a culture capsule. Look at the examples below. Then write an item to represent each of the topics listed in the chart below.

what people do in their free time

a big holiday

TOPICS	ITEMS
school life	
popular food	
a big holiday	
typical clothing	
a traditional custom	
what people do in their free time	
two photographs (of anything)	
other: _____	

B **Group work.** Join another pair. Ask and answer questions about each item. Explain why you chose each one.

Being Different

Lesson B | Adjusting to a new place

1 Vocabulary Link

It's different here.

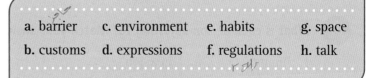

a. barrier   c. environment   e. habits   g. space
b. customs   d. expressions   f. regulations   h. talk

A It can be difficult to adjust to (get used to) a new place. Read about people's experiences. Use the words from the box above to complete the statements.

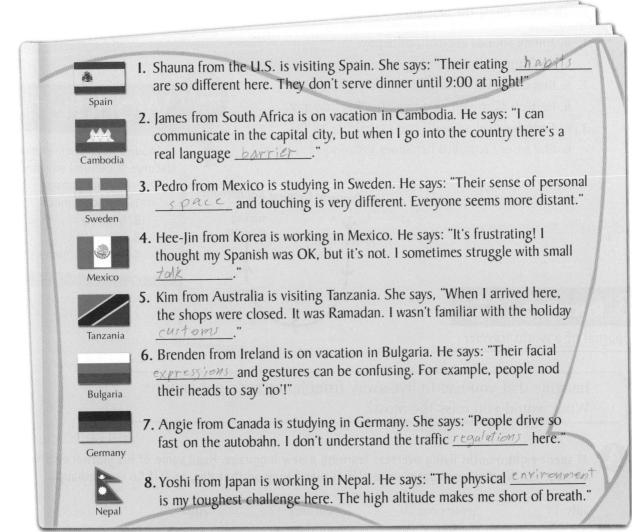

Spain

1. Shauna from the U.S. is visiting Spain. She says: "Their eating _habits_ are so different here. They don't serve dinner until 9:00 at night!"

Cambodia

2. James from South Africa is on vacation in Cambodia. He says: "I can communicate in the capital city, but when I go into the country there's a real language _barrier_."

Sweden

3. Pedro from Mexico is studying in Sweden. He says: "Their sense of personal _space_ and touching is very different. Everyone seems more distant."

Mexico

4. Hee-Jin from Korea is working in Mexico. He says: "It's frustrating! I thought my Spanish was OK, but it's not. I sometimes struggle with small _talk_."

Tanzania

5. Kim from Australia is visiting Tanzania. She says, "When I arrived here, the shops were closed. It was Ramadan. I wasn't familiar with the holiday _customs_."

Bulgaria

6. Brenden from Ireland is on vacation in Bulgaria. He says: "Their facial _expressions_ and gestures can be confusing. For example, people nod their heads to say 'no'!"

Germany

7. Angie from Canada is studying in Germany. She says: "People drive so fast on the autobahn. I don't understand the traffic _regulations_ here."

Nepal

8. Yoshi from Japan is working in Nepal. He says: "The physical _environment_ is my toughest challenge here. The high altitude makes me short of breath."

B Pair work. Use these questions to interview a partner.

1. What are your typical eating habits?
2. What do you do when you encounter a language barrier?
3. Are you a private or public person? How do you feel about personal space?
4. What holiday customs does your family have?
5. Are you good at small talk?
6. Do you typically make a lot of facial expressions?
7. What traffic regulation would you like to change?
8. What's the ideal physical environment and climate for you? Describe the weather.

2 Listening

The first day

Do you remember having difficulty adjusting to a new place? What happened?

 A What is each person adjusting to? Match your answers. (CD 1, Track 33)

1. Jimmy   a. a new job
2. Ben   b. a new school
3. Carly   c. life in a foreign country

 B Listen again. Circle the best answer to complete each statement. (CD 1, Track 34)

1. a. Jimmy sounds excited / ~~unhappy~~.
   b. He learned about ~~holiday customs~~ / personal space.
2. a. Ben used his ~~telephone~~ / computer.
   b. He feels ~~positive~~ / negative after his first day.
3. a. Carly has had a ~~good~~ / bad experience so far.
   b. She ~~wore~~ / removed her shoes indoors.

World Link

Studies have discovered a
U-curve of cultural adjustment
with four phases:
1. the honeymoon
2. hostility
3. humor
4. feeling at home

U-Curve of Cultural Adjustment

honeymoon

hostility

feeling at home

humor

3 Reading

Journal of a world traveler

Imagine that you had to live away from home for eight months. What would you miss the most?

 A JT spent eight months living overseas learning a new language. Read some of his journal entries on page 53. Next to each date, write *H* if JT was happy on that day, or *U* if he was unhappy.

July 14 ___   September 18 ___   February 17 ___   April 20 ___
August 1 ___   December 31 ___   February 27 ___

 B Read the journal entries again. It was hard for JT to adjust to many things. Match each item JT struggled with to a date in the journal. Write the date.

1. change in routine   3. homesickness   5. relationships with friends
       July 14   _____   _____

2. climate   4. language and conversation
   _____   _____

Dear Diary:

July 14: I've been here about a month. It's harder than I thought. First of all, it's very hot and humid and there's no air conditioning. I have less energy and I sleep all the time. I had to give up playing tennis and jogging because it's just too uncomfortable outside. That was hard because I love my exercise routine!

August 1: There's such a language barrier. I try to communicate with gestures and facial expressions. It doesn't usually work very well. I feel like a four-year-old child! Well, one thing is for sure . . . I have to study more!

September 18: Yesterday I went to the movies with some friends. I could actually understand some of it! Everyone here has been very patient with me and my poor language skills. I'm having a great time here!

December 31: Tomorrow is New Year's Day, but I won't be celebrating. I've been sick for about a week. I feel so homesick. I miss my friends and family. People here are nice, but they don't really know me. Sometimes I feel like I'm pretending to be someone else. It's like I have two different personalities . . . one for home and one for here.

February 17: Tomorrow I go home! Guess what, I don't want to go! As soon as I get home, I'll probably want to come right back here!

February 27: Well, I'm at home, but it doesn't feel like home. No one seems very interested in my experiences overseas. My friends just want to engage in small talk. It seems so unimportant. Have I changed or has this place changed?

April 20: I'm starting a new job tomorrow and I'm very excited about it. I'm back into my exercise routine and feeling pretty good. I'm already planning my next big trip . . .

C **Read and circle** *True* **or** *False*.

1.	The summer weather was a little cool.	True	**False**
2.	JT had only basic language skills when he arrived.	**True**	False
3.	He made progress in his language study.	**True**	False
4.	He had fun on New Year's Eve.	True	**False**
5.	JT's friends at home asked him many questions about his trip.	True	**False**
6.	JT felt good about his new job.	**True**	False
7.	He'll probably travel somewhere again soon.	**True**	False

ask&
ANSWER

Describe your daily routine. Could you change it easily? Why or why not?

Future time clauses with *before, after, as soon as, when,* and *while*

 A Study the sentences in the box below. Each sentence contains a future time clause (in blue) and a main clause (in black). Then complete the sentences below.

> Before Alejandro takes the TOEFL exam, he'll study hard.
>
> After I get a job, I'll look for an apartment.
>
> As soon as John arrives in Rio, he's going to the beach.
>
> My mother will call you when your package arrives.
>
> While we wait for the guests, I'll set the table.

1. Words like *before, after,* and *while* appear in the time clause / main clause.

2. The present tense is used in the time clause / main clause.

3. A future verb form appears in the time clause / main clause.

B Alejandro is planning to apply to the University of Southern California (UCLA).
Look at this timeline of his future plans. Then connect the phrases below to make sentences with a future time clause and a main clause.

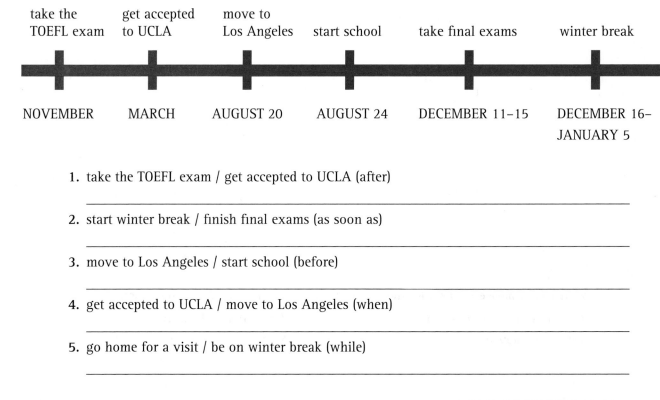

1. take the TOEFL exam / get accepted to UCLA (after)

   _____

2. start winter break / finish final exams (as soon as)

   _____

3. move to Los Angeles / start school (before)

   _____

4. get accepted to UCLA / move to Los Angeles (when)

   _____

5. go home for a visit / be on winter break (while)

   _____

 C Tell a partner about something you plan to do in the future.
Say what you will do before, during, and after the event.

> *I'm planning to go to a concert this weekend with my friends. Before I go, I'm going to . . .*

5 Writing

A language barrier

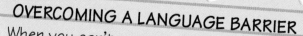

OVERCOMING A LANGUAGE BARRIER
When you can't communicate in the same language easily, it's important to speak slowly. You don't have to speak louder, just more clearly. You can also draw pictures. For example, I use pictures . . .

A Imagine you want to communicate with someone who doesn't speak your language well. What strategies can you use? Add four ideas to the list below.

Speak very slowly   _____   _____

Draw pictures   _____   _____

B Write about ways to overcome a language barrier. Use the ideas listed in **A**.

C Pair work. Exchange papers with a partner. Rank your partner's ideas from most to least effective.

6 Communication

Help for the homesick

A Read about these four people's difficulties living abroad. What advice would you give each person?

"I'm very independent, but I'm alone here. I don't know anyone. There are unfamiliar faces everywhere, and I feel isolated."
– Russell in Europe

"I studied before I came here, but I can't communicate with anyone very well. I don't know how to improve my language skills."
– Julia in Africa

"People here are nice, but I'm homesick. I miss my family and friends."
– Clara in North America

"I like the food here, but I only know about two or three dishes. I'm always eating the same thing!"
– Chris in Asia

B Read the list of advice for people who are homesick. Add your own ideas to the list.

1. Get away. Take a little trip.
2. Go to the movies.
3. Take a cooking class.
4. Invite people to your home.
5. I'd say, "Life at home can be hard, too."
6. Try to talk to little kids.
7. Volunteer somewhere.
8. I'd say, "Your feelings will pass soon."
9. _____
10. _____

C Pair work. Choose a piece of advice for each person.

 Check out the World Link video. **Practice your English online at worldlink.heinle.com.**

6 Big Business

Lesson A | Success stories

1 Vocabulary Link

International companies

A These people are talking about their companies. Read what they say. Notice the words in blue.

This company employs 500 people. We manage three ofices in three different countries.

We produce millior of computer games and ship them to many countries.

Our customers want new products. To compete with other companies, we must work to develop new products first.

We advertise usinç TV commercials ar the Internet. You c purchase our prod in stores or online

B Use the correct form of the words in blue from A to complete the sentences below.

1. Starbucks _produces_ and sells bottled coffee drinks. They also _____ coffee from farmers and sell it in their stores. Starbucks has over 5,500 stores and _____ thousands of people worldwide.

2. Microsoft _____ software and Internet technology for computer users. They _____ their products to Europe, Asia, and Latin America. They _____ branch offices in more than 60 countries.

3. In 1971, Nike was a young company. Its owners paid a struggling designer only $35 for their famous "swoosh" logo. Today they use the logo to _____ their products and to _____ with other sports and fitness companies worldwide.

ask& **ANSWER**

What do you know about the companies in B? What are the advantages or disadvantages of having international companies like these in your country?

2 Listening

First-class businessman

A Listen to this profile of a successful businessman. Who is he? What company does he run? (CD 1, Track 35)

name: _____

company: _____

B Listen again. What different kinds of businesses are mentioned in the profile? (CD 1, Track 36)

1. ☐ air travel 3. ☐ bridal services 5. ☐ modeling 7. ☐ financial services

2. ☐ hotel industry 4. ☐ music 6. ☐ sports 8. ☐ publishing

ask&
ANSWER
What famous businessman or businesswoman do you know? What is he or she known for?

3 Pronunciation

Stress on nouns and verbs with the same spelling

A Listen and repeat the following sentences. Note where the stress falls in the underlined words. (CD 1, Track 37)

NOUN: He gave me a beautiful <u>PREsent</u>.

VERB: Tomorrow I will <u>preSENT</u> my ideas to the board of directors.

B Listen to these sentences. Then practice saying them. (CD 1, Track 38)

NOUN	VERB
1. a. I buy my produce at the market.	b. We produce stereos and CD players.
2. a. No one buys records anymore.	b. I like to record my voice and listen to it.
3. a. I can't deliver it without an address.	b. You need to address the envelope.

C Pair work. Use one of the words from A or B in a sentence as a noun or a verb. Can your partner tell you which it is?

World Link

Coffee is the second most widely traded item in the world (behind petroleum). An estimated 7 million tons are produced every year.

4 Speaking

Tell me about your company.

A Listen to this interview with a successful businesswoman.
Underline the expressions she uses to talk about approximate amounts. (CD 1, Track 39)

Host:	So, welcome to our show. Why don't you tell our listeners who you are and what you do.
Woman:	My name is Beverly Smith. I'm the CEO for TalkBack Communications.
Host:	Can you tell us about your company?
Woman:	Certainly. Our company was founded in 1995. We're based in New York City. We have about 10,000 employees worldwide.
Host:	What does your company do?
Woman:	We do business in a large number of fields, such as telecommunications and computers. Our main area of business is new cell phone technology.
Host:	I hear your company is doing quite well.
Woman:	Well, we made over five million dollars profit last year. Experts say our company will grow by up to 10% next year.

B Pair work. Practice the conversation with a partner.

5 Speaking Strategy

Talking about approximate amounts

A Create your own company and complete a company profile for it.

B Pair work. Role play. Play the parts of a TV host and a business professional. Ask and answer questions about your companies. Use the Useful Expressions to help you.

Company Profile

Name of company: _____
Location: _____
Number of employees: _____
Fields you work in: _____
_____
Main industry: _____
Current projects: _____
_____
Profit/loss in past year: _____
Growth prospect for next year: _____
_____

> What's your current project?

> We're developing a new kind of camera. We've been working on this project for nearly two years!

Useful Expressions:
Talking about approximate amounts

Approximately 400 employees work here.

The average worker earns **about** $20,000 per year.

We have **a large number of** opportunities to expand our business.

We spent **nearly** three months on the project.

Our profits will decline **over** two percent this year.

You can save **up to** 50% if you buy it now.

6 Language Link

Passive voice: the simple present and the simple past

A Read this company profile.

MTV was launched on August 1, 1981. A video called "Video Killed the Radio Star" was shown first. MTV was not very popular in the beginning. That changed, however, when Michael Jackson's videos were played by the network.

In 1985, MTV started a second video channel, VH1. In the 1990s, MTV Asia, MTV Latino, and MTV Russia were started.

Today MTV is a worldwide success story. It still shows music videos. Other programs are broadcast by MTV as well. MTV is consistently voted one of the most popular TV stations by young TV viewers.

B Notice the two passive voice sentences highlighted above. Which sentence is in the present and which is in the past? How is the passive formed? Can you find other examples of each?

C Put the verbs in parentheses into the present or past passive to complete this company profile. What company is it? Check your answer on page 154.

David Filo and Jerry Yang: founders of the company

HISTORY OF THE COMPANY

This company (1. start) __was__ originally __started__ as a hobby by two students in 1994. In the beginning it (2. call) _____ _____ "Jerry and David's Guide to the World Wide Web." Their product (3. place) _____ _____ on two computers. The computers (4. name) _____ _____ after two sumo wrestlers. The company grew quickly. Many stories (5. broadcast) _____ _____ about it in the 1990s.

THE COMPANY TODAY

This company's Internet destination (6. visit) __is__ __visited__ by millions of people worldwide. It (7. used) _____ _____ to find information. Free e-mail services (8. offer) _____ _____ , too. Most of its profit (9. provide) _____ _____ by advertising. Its main offices (10. find) _____ _____ in California.

D Group work. Brainstorm a list of big companies you know.
Write down some information about one of the companies on your list.
Then describe your company to the class and see if they can guess its name.

> The company was started by an Englishwoman. They make cosmetics. I really like their grapefruit shampoo.

> Is it The Body Shop?

A Look at this profile of Iceland. How is Iceland different from your country?

Iceland

geyser

Name of country: Republic of Iceland
Capital city: Reykjavik
Population: 279,384 (2002 est.)
Literacy rate: 100%
Nature: hot springs, canyons, glaciers
Products: cattle, sheep, fish,
                  potatoes, turnips
Industry: aluminum
Imports: machinery, foodstuffs

sheep

glaciers

aluminum

B On a separate piece of paper, write down a list
of facts about Iceland. Use active and passive
sentences. You can use the verbs below to help you.

| find | grow | import | produce | raise |

FACTS ABOUT ICELAND

*The population is approxima
280,000. Up to 100% of the pe
can read. Many hot springs
are found . . .*

 C Pair work. With a partner, make up a list of facts about your city, region, or country. Include at least
six interesting facts and some passive sentences. Then present your list of facts to the class.

Big Business

Lesson B | The ABCs of advertising

1 Vocabulary Link

Popular products

A Look at how different products are advertised. Then match the type of advertising with its picture.

> a. billboard   c. bumper sticker   e. poster   g. TV commercial
> b. brochure   d. junk mail   f. skywriting   h. window display

1.
2.
3.
4.
5.
6.
7.
8.

B Pair work. Find out what kinds of advertisements your partner notices during a typical day. Report your findings back to the class.

> *Let's see . . . I get up at 7 a.m. Sometimes I watch television before I go to school.*

> *So then you see some TV commercials in the morning, right?*

 ask&
ANSWER

What kinds of people would be attracted to each ad in A?
What kind of advertising is most eye-catching to you? Why?

A Look at these objects. What do you think they are used for? Check (✓) the correct box for each item.

☐ for fixing cars

☐ for mountain climbing

☐ for writing

☐ for trimming hair

☐ for relaxing

☐ for celebrating

☐ for making holes

☐ for opening bottles

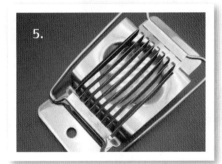

☐ for slicing food

☐ for sharpening knives

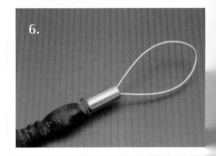

☐ for cleaning tongues

☐ for catching animals

 B Now listen to a quiz show to check your answers. (CD 1, Track 40)

 **World** Link

The average American sees or hears about 600 advertisements a day. By age 65, he or she will have seen over 2 million TV ads.

3 Reading

Is advertising necessary?

A Group work. Complete these two statements and then discuss them as a group.

1. There is _____ advertising in our society.   **a.** too much   **b.** just the right amount of

2. Advertising is _____ to sell products.   **a.** necessary   **b.** not necessary

B Read the article below. Compare your answers in A with the author's opinion.

Ad or no ad?

Is advertising really necessary? Billions of dollars are spent on it every year, so it must be important. After all, it's a busy world. You have to advertise, sell products, and make money!

Not every company thinks that way. The NO-AD company ("no-ad" stands for "not advertised") avoids big advertising campaigns. The company was started in 1960 and is successful today. Their products are still affordable because the company saves money on advertising. They also use their savings to support a drug and alcohol awareness program to educate high school students.

NO-AD sells by word of mouth. "Word-of-mouth advertising" happens when a person tells another person about a good experience with a product or service. That second person then tells another friend, family member, or colleague. And so a chain of information is created.

Typically, advertisers talk about how good their product is. Although they say things like, "Studies show that our product is the best," or "Everyone loves this product," it can sound insincere or unconvincing. It's much more believable to hear about a product from someone who did not make it. Our friends' opinions are very important to us, so we often listen to their advice about a product.

Word-of-mouth advertising has other advantages, too. It's cost-effective (after all, it's free) and a company doesn't have to create a complex business plan to do it. Here is some advice for small businesses about word-of-mouth advertising:

- Be prepared to talk about your company at any time. You never know who you will meet. Always carry business cards.
- Only say positive things about your company. Don't say negative things about your competition.
- Help other companies by referring people to them. The more you help others, the more good fortune will come back to you.

C How does the author feel about word–of–mouth advertising and paid–media advertising? Write down your ideas in the chart below.

WORD-OF-MOUTH ADVERTISING	PAID MEDIA ADVERTISING (RADIO, TV, ETC.)
It's free.	

ANSWER

There are many different types of advertising. Which method do you think is best?

Connecting words: *because, so, although*

A Look at this advertisement. Find the connecting words.

WHITER & BRIGHTER
LAUNDRY DETERGENT

More people are using new and
improved *Whiter & Brighter*
because it really works!

We know that you love your
old brand. Well, it can't beat
Whiter & Brighter even though
it may do a good job.

Millions of customers are trying it,
so why don't you try it too!

"Although I have a big,
messy family, everyone looks clean!
I love Whiter & Brighter!"

"Because I get dirty at work,
I use Whiter & Brighter to clean
all my clothes!"

B Answer the questions.

1. Which connecting word(s) can be placed at the beginning or in the middle of a sentence?
2. Which connecting word(s) follow a comma?

C Use the connecting words to join together these sentences.

1. I hate TV commercials. I don't watch television. (so)

_____

2. We can't advertise on TV. It's expensive. (because)

_____

3. Advertising on TV is very expensive. Companies still do it. (although)

_____

D Which connecting words in C . . .

1. introduce a clause that gives a reason? _____
2. introduce a clause that shows a result? _____
3. introduce a clause with a surprising result? _____

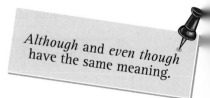

Although and *even though*
have the same meaning.

E Complete the sentences below with *although/even though, because,* **and** *so.* **Then explain your choices.**

1. The advertising campaign was successful, _____so_____ many people bought the product.
2. People say word-of-mouth advertising is cost-effective _____ it's free.
3. _____ their product is affordable, it doesn't work as well as ours.
4. The new toy was very popular, _____ all the stores quickly sold out of it.
5. _____ it increases their sales, many companies spend money on advertising.

5 Writing

Consumer advice

A You have been asked to write a review for a magazine. Choose an item you have bought recently and write about its good and bad qualities.

B Share your writing with a partner. Talk about the item's good and bad points.

6 Communication

Rate the advertisement.

THIS PRODUCT IS RATED: ☆☆☆☆☆

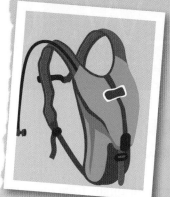

I like to go mountain biking. When it's hot, I often stop to drink water. I like to use my Hydro-Pak because I can ride and drink at the same time! The Hydro-Pak has a hose connected to a water container inside. It's convenient and lightweight. It comes in many different colors, so I'm sure you can find one you like.

A Group work. Read these popular advertising slogans. Complete each one with a word from the box. What kind of product or service do you think each one was used for?

driving   flowers   ~~milk~~   news   skies   world

1. "Got __milk__?"
2. "Say it with _____."
3. "Fly the friendly _____."
4. "All the _____ that's fit to print."
5. "The ultimate _____ machine."
6. "Give us 20 minutes and we'll give you the _____."

B Group work. Each person in the group thinks of another well-known print advertisement. On a separate piece of paper, sketch the ad or make an ad of your own.

C Group work. Present your ad to the group. Your classmates will use the checklist below to rate your ad.

	Yes	No
1. Is the slogan easy to remember?	○	○
2. Is the ad eye-catching?	○	○
3. Is the message positive?	○	○
4. Is the design simple and clean?	○	○
5. Is the ad original?	○	○
6. What do you like most about this ad? _____		
7. Would you buy this product? Why or why not? _____		

 Check out the World Link video.

 Practice your English online at worldlink.heinle.com.

1 Storyboard

 A Al is always borrowing things from his friend Manny. Look at the pictures and complete the conversation. More than one answer is possible for each blank.

 B Pair work. Practice the conversation. Then change roles and practice again.

A Pair work. Look at these pictures of Bev and Dan. Then answer the questions.

- How would you describe Bev and Dan?
- How do they feel about each other?
- Where are they in each situation? How are they dressed?
- In the first picture, what do you think Dan is saying to Bev?
- In the second situation, what are they doing? What do you think they are talking about?

B Pair work. On a separate piece of paper, write a conversation for each situation. Then act the conversations out.

3 The cultural iceberg

 A Read about the cultural iceberg. Circle the correct answers.

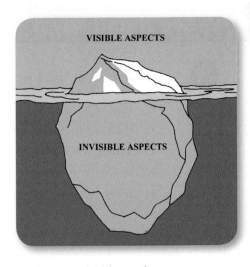

VISIBLE ASPECTS

INVISIBLE ASPECTS

   Culture is similar to an iceberg. There are aspects that are visible and invisible. Most of our cultural values are hidden. For example, when you visit a restaurant in Japan, people often sit on the floor. This eating habit / facial expression is obvious. You may not know, however, that while it's inappropriate / appropriate for men to sit cross-legged, it is atypical / typical for women to do so.

   You can see that many Americans are open and friendly. However, there's a hidden rule: you shouldn't ask about salary. It's considered impolite / polite and some people find it inoffensive / offensive.

 B Complete the chart with *dos* and *don'ts* (the rules of behavior) from your culture.

	Eating habits	Holiday customs	Traffic regulations
Dos			
Don'ts			

 C Class activity. Share your cultural dos and don'ts with the class.

4 Listening: Are you Mr. Right?

Find Your Man!

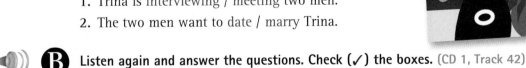 **A** A host is talking to some guests on a TV show called "Find Your Man!" Listen and then circle the best words to complete the statements. (CD 1, Track 41)

1. Trina is interviewing / meeting two men.
2. The two men want to date / marry Trina.

B Listen again and answer the questions. Check (✓) the boxes. (CD 1, Track 42)

	Guest 1	Guest 2
1. Who likes sports?	☐	☐
2. Who left his date in the restaurant?	☐	☐
3. Who doesn't live alone?	☐	☐
4. Who has never dated before?	☐	☐
5. Who is unemployed?	☐	☐
6. Who thinks he's talented?	☐	☐

C Pair work. Compare your answers with a partner.
Would either of these men be a good date for Trina? Why or why not?

5 That annoys me.

A Match the words to make appropriate compound words. For some words, more than one combination is possible.

__C__ 1. blind   a. commercials
_____ 2. holiday   b. customs
_____ 3. junk   c. dates
_____ 4. plastic   d. mail
_____ 5. traffic   e. regulations
_____ 6. TV   f. surgery

B Pair work. Discuss and answer these questions about the noun combinations in A. Explain your answers.

1. Which ones annoy you?
2. Which ones do you enjoy?
3. Which ones do you avoid?

6 The Taj Mahal and Ayer's Rock

A Read the sentences and then check the ones that are passive.

1. ☐ It is a famous site in India.
2. ☐ It is also known by the name Uluru.
3. ☐ It is located in the middle of Australia.
4. ☐ It is made of white marble.

5. ☐ It takes three hours to climb to the top.
6. ☐ It was built by Shah Jehan as a memorial to his wife.
7. ☐ It was finished by 1648.

B Which sentences in A describe each picture? Write the numbers of the sentences in A under the pictures below. Then check your answers on page 154.

_____   _____

C Think of a famous place. Write five or six sentences about the place on a sheet of paper. Some of your sentences should be in the passive.

D Pair work. Take turns reading sentences with your partner. Try and guess your partner's place.

World Link

Developing
English
Fluency

Susan Stempleski

James R. Morgan • Nancy Douglas

Kristin Johannsen

HEINLE
CENGAGE Learning

World Link, Combo Split 3A
Susan Stempleski
James R. Morgan, Nancy Douglas,
Kristin Johannesen

Publisher: Christopher Wenger
Director of Content Development:
Anita Raducanu
Director of Product Marketing: Amy Mabley
Acquisitions Editor: Mary Sutton-Paul
Developmental Editor: Paul MacIntyre,
Jean Pender, Rebbecca Klevberg
Content Project Manager: Tan Jin Hock
Sr. Print Buyer: Mary Beth Hennebury
International Marketing Manager:
Eric Brederberg
Compositor: CHROME Media Pte. Ltd.
Illustrator: Raketshop Design Studio
(Philippines)
Cover/Text Designer: CHROME Media Pte. Ltd.
Cover Images: CHROME Media Pte. Ltd.
PhotoDisc, Inc.
Photo Credits
Unless otherwise stated, all photos are from PhotoDisc, Inc.
Digital Imagery © copyright 2005 PhotoDisc, Inc. and TYA Inc.
Photos from other sources: page 12: (top) Gilles Mingasson/
Getty Images, (bottom) Susumu Takahashi/Reuters/Landov;
page 27: Peter Turnley/CORBIS

Every effort has been made to trace all sources of illustrations/photos/information in this book, but if any have been inadvertently overlooked, the publisher will be pleased to make the necessary arrangements at the first opportunity.

ISBN-13: 978-1-4130-1086-2

ISBN-10: 1-4130-1086-5

Heinle
25 Thomson Place
Boston, Massachusetts 02210
USA

Cengage Learning is a leading provider of customized learning solutions with office locations around the globe, including Singapore, the United Kingdom, Australia, Mexico, Brazil and Japan. Locate our local office at:
international.cengage.com/region

Cengage Learning products are represented in Canada by Nelson Education, Ltd.

Visit Heinle online at **elt.heinle.com**
Visit our corporate website at **cengage.com**

1 Vocabulary Workout

 A Complete the sentences with an item from the box.

can opener	frying pan	remote control	smoke detector
swimming pool	vacuum cleaner	washing machine	burglar alarm
air conditioner	barbecue grill	alarm clock	

1. Turn on the _____! It's really hot in here.
2. At our party on Saturday, we cooked chicken and steak outdoors on the _____.
3. I hate the sound of my _____. It wakes me up every morning at 6:00 a.m.
4. I use the _____ to turn my TV on.
5. Chris cooked eggs for breakfast in the _____.
6. The _____ makes a loud noise if there is a fire in your house.
7. When thieves entered the shop at night, the _____ made a loud noise and the police came.
8. Where's the _____? I want to put some canned fruit in this salad.
9. Mr. and Mrs. Park have a big _____ in their backyard. The neighborhood children love to play there.
10. Please put your dirty clothes in the _____. I'm going to do the laundry.
11. Use the _____ to clean the living room carpet.

B Look at the items in **A**. Which three are the most useful for you? Why?

1. Item: _____

   Reason: _____

   _____

2. Item: _____

   Reason: _____

   _____

3. Item: _____

   Reason: _____

   _____

Which one is NOT useful for you? Why?

Item: _____

Reason: _____

_____

2 Conversation Workout

A A realtor is showing a house to Jasmine. Complete the conversation with these phrases.

living room	look at the bedrooms	have a garden	nice and roomy	two-bedroom
I work at home a lot	a room for my home office	go outside	big yard	

Realtor: This is the _____.

Jasmine: It's _____.

Realtor: Yes, there's a lot of room. It's a _____ _____ house.

Jasmine: Great. I need _____ because _____.

Realtor: And there's also a _____.

Jasmine: Great! I'd love to _____.

Realtor: Shall we _____?

Jasmine: Okay.

B What do these people want and need in a house? Write new conversations.

1. Yoshi loves to cook.

Realtor: This is the _____.

Yoshi: It's _____.

Realtor: Yes, there's a lot of room. It's a _____ _____ house.

Yoshi: Great. I need _____ because _____.

Realtor: And there's also a _____.

Yoshi: Great! I'd love to _____.

Realtor: Shall we _____?

2. Mr. and Mrs. Willis have a big family.

Realtor: This is the _____.

Mrs. Willis: It's _____.

Realtor: Yes, there's a lot of room. It's a _____ _____ house.

Mrs. Willis: Great. I need _____ because _____.

Realtor: And there's also a _____.

Mrs. Willis: Great! I'd love to _____.

Realtor: Shall we _____?

Mrs. Willis: Okay.

3 Language Workout

A What is it used for? Write two sentences about each thing. Follow the example.

Example: frying pan   *It's used to cook food.*
                        It's used for cooking food.

1. washing machine   _____.

                       _____.

2. air conditioner   _____.

                       _____.

3. smoke detector   _____.

                       _____.

4. barbecue grill   _____.

                       _____.

5. answering machine   _____.

                       _____.

B Look at the conversation.

Paulo: I'm looking for something, but I don't know what it's called in English.

Ann: What is it used for?

Paulo: It's heavy and it's used for keeping books together.

Ann: Oh, that. It's called a bookend.

C Write similar conversations about these things.

1. You: _____.
   Ann: _____.
   You: _____.
   Ann: _____.

2. You: _____.
   Ann: _____.
   You: _____.
   Ann: _____.

3. You: _____.
   Ann: _____.
   You: _____.
   Ann: _____.

Indoors and Outdoors

Lesson B | Public spaces

1 Vocabulary & Language Workout

A Match the words 1–7 with a–g. Write the letter on the line.

1. bus _____
2. university _____
3. newspaper _____
4. parking _____

a. space
b. campus
c. station
d. entrance

5. subway _____
6. taxi _____
7. traffic _____

e. kiosk
f. light
g. stand

B Complete the sentences with an item from **A**.

1. When I want something to read, I stop at the _____ on my way to work.
2. After the concert, many people were waiting in line at the _____.
3. In my city, it's very difficult to find a _____ downtown.
4. You must always stop when the _____ is red.
5. The _____ in my city is really beautiful, with large trees and very old buildings.
6. You can buy tickets from a machine at the _____.
7. From the _____, you can travel to many parts of my country.

C What are the rules? Write two rules for each situation using expressions from the box.

| can't | (not) be allowed to | mustn't | no _____ing allowed |

1. In a hospital

_____

_____

2. During an exam

_____

_____

3. At a concert

_____

_____

4. At a beach

_____

_____

Ⓐ Find underlined words in the reading with these meanings.

Take Back Your Street!

Two neighbors meet on a city sidewalk. They talk about planting more flowers along their street, or asking the city council to add <u>bike lanes</u> to a busy road. In small but important ways, these people are changing the face of their cities.

All around the world, people are speaking up and working hard to make their cities safer and more pleasant for <u>pedestrians</u>. Cities have painted <u>crosswalks</u> on their streets, made streets narrower, put in traffic lights and <u>speed bumps</u>, and made plans to help more kids walk or bike to school.

Many people have learned from a man from Brisbane, Australia, named David Engwicht. His book *Reclaiming Our Cities and Towns* has a simple message. He says that in the past, streets belonged to everybody. Kids played there, and neighbors stopped there to talk.

But now, streets are just for cars and trucks. People stay inside to get away from the noise and dangerous traffic, and we lose <u>contact</u> with our neighbors. Engwicht says that we should use streets for more than just transportation. People need to take back their streets.

Engwicht travels around the world, helping people think differently about pedestrians, streets, and neighborhoods. Besides his books and articles, he gives many speeches. He has worked in neighborhoods from Honolulu to Scotland.

While Engwicht was writing his book, he learned about how neighbors in the city of Delft, in the Netherlands, stopped dangerous traffic on their street. They put old couches, tables, and <u>planters</u> in the street. Cars could still pass, but they had to drive slowly. When the police arrived, they saw the value of these <u>illegal</u> actions to make the streets safer. Soon city officials started planning ways to make cars slow down, and "<u>calm</u>" the traffic.

Engwicht says we should think about streets as our "outdoor living room." Calming the traffic is just the beginning. In the future, streets will be safe places for children again, and our neighbors will become our friends.

1. to make something quieter   _____

2. places to plant flowers   _____

3. against the law   _____

4. people who are walking   _____

5. special places to go across the street   _____

6. places for people to ride bicycles   _____

7. a little "hill" in a road to make people drive slower   _____

8. communication   _____

B **What would Mr. Engwicht think about these things? Check the answers.**

1. bigger streets   good idea ＿＿   bad idea ＿＿
2. more parks   good idea ＿＿   bad idea ＿＿
3. faster cars   good idea ＿＿   bad idea ＿＿
4. a neighborhood café   good idea ＿＿   bad idea ＿＿
5. more bicycles   good idea ＿＿   bad idea ＿＿

C **Read and circle the correct word.**

There are several ways to improve life in my city. Our
(1: **bigger/biggest**) problem is transportation. We really
need more ways to get around. I'd (2: **like/liking**) to ride my
bicycle to work, but there is too (3: **much/many**) traffic on
the streets. We need (4: **safer/safest**) places for bicycling and
walking. (5: **Another/Other**) problem is the parks. We have
(6: **some/any**) nice parks, but we don't take good care of
them and they are often dirty. We need cleaner parks, where
children can play and adults can relax. One more problem is
nightlife. There's (7: **nothing/anything**) to do in the evening!
We should (8: **build/building**) a big theater for plays and
concerts.

D **Write about how to improve life in your city.**

Life Is All About Change

Lesson A | The times of your life

1 Vocabulary Workout

A Fill in the spaces with the correct form of a word from the box.

adulthood	teenager	senior citizen	old	young	infancy
middle-aged	grown-up	childhood	adult	infant	adolescence

1. Antonio just had his 13th birthday. Now he is a _____.
2. Some movie theaters have cheaper tickets for _____ over age 65.
3. It's great being _____! Your health is good and you have lots of energy.
4. Most _____ people have gray or white hair.
5. _____ is the time from 0–2 years of age.
6. Mi-Ran's youngest child is an _____, only six months old.
7. My uncle Pete is _____. He's about 50 years old.
8. You must be an _____ to vote in this country.
9. _____ is the period when children grow into adults.
10. In Japan, _____ starts at age 20.
11. _____ is a time of playing and learning.
12. My little brother wants to be a _____ so he can stay up late and go to parties!

B Write the words from A in the correct box.

Nouns for people	Nouns for parts of life	Adjectives

C Write an age for each sentence. Use your own ideas.

1. My son is too young to stay home alone in the evening. — Age: _____
2. Mr. Arthur really should retire. Old people shouldn't work so hard. — Age: _____
3. Lucy is getting married! I think she's too young. — Age: _____
4. Tonya wants to quit her job. In my opinion, she's too old to change jobs. — Age: _____
5. Infants should just play and have fun. They're too young for lessons. — Age: _____
6. In my opinion, middle-aged women should stop wearing short skirts. — Age: _____

2 Conversation Workout

A Unscramble the sentences to make a conversation.

(you / what / doing / are)

Jan: _____?

(plane / I'm / a / on / the Internet / ticket / buying)

Mike: _____.

(really / planning / are / you / to / go / where)

Jan: _____? _____?

(to / my friends / I'm / visit / in Spain / going)

Mike: _____.

(what / there / will / do / you)

Jan: _____?

(thinking / we're / about / a car / together / renting)

Mike: _____.

B Now write new conversations. Use the expressions in the box.

planning to   going to   plan to
intend to   thinking about

1. Jason: _____
   Andy: _____
   Jason: _____
   Andy: _____
   Jason: _____
   Andy: _____

2. Cathy: _____
   Miki: _____
   Cathy: _____
   Miki: _____
   Cathy: _____
   Miki: _____

3 Language Workout

A **Which sentences talk about these things in the future? Write the correct letter in the space.**

a. something about to happen
b. a scheduled event
c. a plan or intention
d. a general prediction
e. a decision at the moment of speaking
f. a plan already made

1. On Saturday, we're playing tennis at Metro Park and having a picnic. ____
2. The movie starts at 8:00 in Theater B. ____
3. I'm going to read some books about Japan before I go on vacation there. ____
4. Tomorrow's weather will be sunny and warmer, with a temperature of 25 degrees. ____
5. Oh no! That car's going to crash! ____
6. I'm really hungry. I'll make a sandwich. ____
7. Our English class has a test on Friday. ____
8. In the future, students will take all their classes over the Internet. ____
9. Maria is going to look for a better job this year. ____
10. Please close the windows. It's going to rain. ____

B **Complete the e-mail with a future form of the verb.**

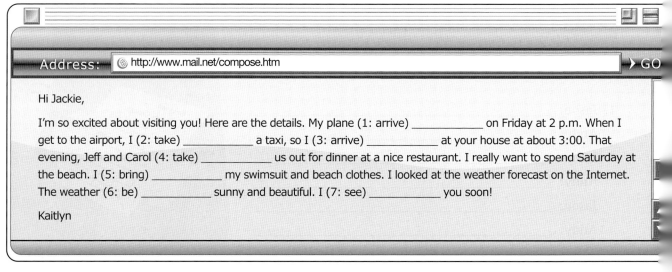

Address: ⊕ http://www.mail.net/compose.htm ▸ GO

Hi Jackie,

I'm so excited about visiting you! Here are the details. My plane (1: arrive) _____ on Friday at 2 p.m. When I get to the airport, I (2: take) _____ a taxi, so I (3: arrive) _____ at your house at about 3:00. That evening, Jeff and Carol (4: take) _____ us out for dinner at a nice restaurant. I really want to spend Saturday at the beach. I (5: bring) _____ my swimsuit and beach clothes. I looked at the weather forecast on the Internet. The weather (6: be) _____ sunny and beautiful. I (7: see) _____ you soon!

Kaitlyn

C **Now write your own sentences.**

1. What are your plans for next weekend?

_____

_____

2. What are your predictions for 100 years from now?

People _____

_____

3. What is the schedule for next week's English class?

_____

_____

Life Is All About Change

Lesson B | Milestones

1 Vocabulary & Language Workout

A Match the sentence parts. Write the letter of the answer on the line.

1. If you get promoted, _____
2. When people get divorced, _____
3. When older people retire, _____
4. If you move out, _____
5. When you graduate, _____
6. When two people fall in love, _____

a. you finish your studies at a school.
b. they stop being husband and wife.
c. you go to live in a new place.
d. they want to spend all their time together.
e. they become husband and wife.
f. you have a better job at your company.

B When do these life changes usually happen? Write them in the correct box.

retire
get married
graduate from high school
fall in love
move out from your parents' house
get your first job

get a driver's license
get divorced
have a baby
become a grandparent
graduate from elementary school
get a promotion

Childhood	Adolescence	Adulthood	Old age

C What are you going to do at these times? Write two sentences with may/might/could or may not/might not. Follow the example.

1. Next month _____

_____

2. Next summer _____

_____

3. Next year _____

_____

4. In five years _____

_____

A Read the web site.

Celebrating Life Changes

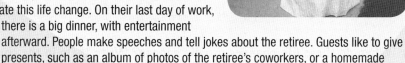

*I*n Mexico and some other Latin American countries, girls mark their fifteenth birthday with a celebration called the *Quinceanera*. In the morning, the birthday girl goes to church with her family and her best friends. She wears a beautiful (and sometimes very expensive!) dress. Later in the day, there is a huge party, with a big cake that matches the girl's dress, and a night filled with music and dancing.

When older people in the United States retire, their friends and coworkers often give them a retirement party to celebrate this life change. On their last day of work, there is a big dinner, with entertainment afterward. People make speeches and tell jokes about the retiree. Guests like to give presents, such as an album of photos of the retiree's coworkers, or a homemade video of the retiree's friends.

Becoming an adult is a very important life change, and Japan has a special holiday to celebrate this. The second Sunday in January is Coming-of-Age Day. On that day, everyone who had their twentieth birthday in the last year goes to their town's City Hall for a special ceremony. Everyone dresses up, and many women wear beautiful kimonos. The mayor makes a speech and gives presents to all the new adults.

Some kids are afraid to start school, but six-year-olds in Germany can't wait. For them, *Schulanfang* is a big holiday. To celebrate a child's first day of school, parents or friends give the child a *Zuckertuete*, a big colorful cardboard cone filled with candy and little presents. People take pictures of the kids holding their *Zuckertuete*, and there is a school party later for the parents, with cake and coffee.

B Complete the chart with information from the reading.

Mexico			Japan	
Quinceanera				*Schulanfang*
		second Sunday in January		
	people who are retiring			six-year-old children
		dress up, go to City Hall, hear a speech,		
		get presents		

C Fill in a future form of the verb.

My sister **(1: get)** _____ married in May. We're really busy planning the wedding now! The ceremony **(2: be)** _____ at 2:00 in the afternoon. After that, we **(3: have)** _____ a party at a restaurant. Next week, we **(4: look)** _____ for a band to play music at the party. After the wedding, my sister and her husband **(5: go)** _____ on their honeymoon. They **(6: plan)** _____ to go to Hawaii, because the weather **(7: be)** _____ very good. I think it **(8: be)** _____ a beautiful wedding.

D Write about a happy change in your life—in the past or the future.

_____

_____

_____

_____

_____

_____

_____

_____

_____

Newspapers and the News

Lesson A | The people behind the news

1 Vocabulary Workout

Solve this crossword puzzle with the vocabulary from the unit.

The Latest News

Across

4. If your job is _____, it's the same every day.
6. A _____ sends stories from another place to the newspaper.
7. finding out and telling about the news
9. A _____ checks and corrects newspaper articles.
10. A _____ draws funny pictures for a newspaper.

Down

1. This person writes stories for a newspaper.
2. If you _____ a person, you ask many questions.
3. This person reads the news from a TV studio. (two words)
5. in more than one country
8. A _____ manages and publishes a newspaper.
9. A _____ writes opinions about movies, concerts, and books.

4. P R E D I C T A B L E

7. J O U R N A L I S M

2 Conversation Workout

A Match the sentence parts to make questions. Write the letter of the answer on the line.

1. Who ____
2. Do you ____
3. Is ____
4. Do you know ____
5. Can you tell ____

a. know the reporter?
b. is the reporter?
c. me who the reporter is?
d. who the reporter is?
e. that the reporter?

B Now use the expressions in A to write a different question for each of these people.

1. the bank robber _____
2. the tennis champion _____
3. Dr. Sanchez _____
4. the newspaper editor _____
5. Professor Graves _____

C Your teacher is sick one day, and a new teacher comes to your class.
Write conversations about students in your class.

1. Teacher: Hello, I'm Brad Sato. I'm your teacher today.
   You: _____, Mr. Sato.
   Teacher: I have a paper for _____. Who is he/she?
   You: (He/She) is sitting over there.
   Teacher: Is (he/she) _____?
   You: No, that's _____. _____ is _____
   _____.

2. Teacher: Hello, my name In-Sook Lee. I'm teaching your class today.
   You: _____, Ms. Lee.
   Teacher: I have a paper for _____. _____?
   You: (He/She) is _____.
   Teacher: Is (he/she) _____?
   You: No, that's _____. _____ is _____
   _____.

3. Teacher: Hello, I'm Marcus Collins. I'm teaching your class today.
   You: _____, Mr. Collins.
   Teacher: I have a paper for _____. _____?
   You: (He/She) is _____.
   Teacher: Is (he/she) _____?
   You: No, that's _____. _____ is _____
   _____.

3 Language Workout

1. (who / do / know / the / you / actor / is) _____?
   (long hair / he's / the guy / with / the) _____.
2. (can / who / you / tell / the photographer / me / is) _____?
   (woman / she's / camera bag / carrying / the / the) _____.
3. (do / know / news anchor / the / you) _____?
   (in / the / one / the blue suit / he's) _____.
4. (who / sports reporter / the / is) _____?
   (typing / he's / man / on / the / laptop / his) _____.

B These women are quintuplets—five sisters born at the same time. Write three sentences about each woman. Follow the example.

1. Do you know who Jan is?
   Jan's the one holding a tennis racket.
   She's the one in _____
   _____

2. Can you tell me who Lisa is?
   Lisa _____
   _____

3. Can you tell me who Sara is?
   Sara _____
   _____

4. Is that Anne?
   Anne _____
   _____

5. Do you know who Beth is?
   Beth _____
   _____

Newspapers and the News

Lesson B | In the news

1 Vocabulary & Language Workout

A Match the words and their meanings. Write the letter of the answer on the line.

1. comics _____
2. daily _____
3. headlines _____
4. scan _____
5. horoscope _____
6. published _____
7. sections _____
8. sensational _____
9. subscribe _____
10. weather forecast _____

a. predictions about temperature, rain, etc.
b. parts of a newspaper
c. pay money to receive a newspaper every day
d. the day's predictions for your star sign
e. shocking and surprising
f. printed and sold to people
g. every day
h. titles of newspaper articles
i. funny stories in words and pictures
j. to read very quickly for the important ideas

B What's in the newspaper? Write as many things as you can.

Daily	Sometimes

C Fill in the correct form of the verb (simple past or present perfect).

1. Since we (start) _____ World Link 3, we (finish) _____ two units.

2. I (eat) _____ at Mario's Restaurant many times. I (go) _____ there last week with my roommate.

3. Jessica (live) _____ in her apartment since October. Before that, she (live) _____ with her parents.

4. The weather (be) _____ rainy again yesterday. It (be) _____ rainy every day for a long time!

5. Elias (be, not) _____ to the United States, but he (go) _____ to Canada in 2003.

6. I (know) _____ my best friend since we (be) _____ ten years old.

7. Since I (come) _____ to this school, I (meet) _____ a lot of nice people.

A Read the newspaper articles and write the correct headline for each article. Two headlines are extra.

A Dangerous Occupation	They Couldn't Communicate	Beautiful Girls
Silent Beauties	Robbery at Store	A Very Busy Thief

News Daily, Jun 24

1. _____

A bank robbery in Virginia, USA, was stopped when the robber and the bank teller couldn't reach an agreement. The robber pushed a holdup note under the window, but the teller looked at it, said, "I can't read this," and gave it back. The robber pushed the note through a second time. The teller crumpled the note up and threw it at the robber. He picked it up and walked out of the bank.

2. _____

A professional ice hockey player will miss the rest of this season's games because he injured himself. National Hockey League goalie Jean-Louis Blanchard went on the injured list after he fell and seriously hurt his back. He was walking out of a restaurant in Ottawa, Canada, when he slipped on some ice.

3. _____

The first international camel beauty contest was held last week in Alxa, in western China. More than 100 dressed-up camels entered the contest. The judges examined them for shiny hair, tall humps, and beautiful costumes. Unlike human beauty contests, though, there were no interviews with the contestants.

4. _____

Police in Sheffield, England, arrested a 41-year-old man for stealing five cars. Graham Owens went to car dealers and said he wanted to buy a car, and borrowed a car to test-drive. Each time, he drove the car around, then cleaned it inside and washed it outside—before leaving it at the side of the road, and walking home.

B Match these words from the reading with their meanings. Write the letter of the answer on the line.

1. teller ____
2. crumple ____
3. injure ____
4. seriously ____
5. examine ____
6. hump ____
7. contestant ____
8. dealer ____

a. hurt
b. crush out of shape as with paper
c. look at carefully
d. someone who tries to win a prize
e. a person who sells something
f. badly
g. a bank employee
h. a shape like a hill

C Read this article from a school newspaper and fill in the correct form of the verb (simple past or present perfect).

Mr. Bryan Gale is one of the most interesting teachers at Capitol Institute. He **(1: teach)** _____ here since 1999. Before that, he **(2: work)** _____ at an international school. He **(3: have)** _____ many different jobs in his life. After he **(4: graduate)** _____ from university, he **(5: start)** _____ working for the city government. Later, he **(6: become)** _____ a TV reporter. But after ten years, he **(7: be)** _____ tired of television. He **(8: go)** _____ back to university and **(9: study)** _____ to become a teacher. He **(10: be)** _____ an English teacher for ten years now, and he **(11: write)** _____ four books for students. Many people **(12: buy)** _____ Mr. Gale's books because they are really funny, and very useful.

D Write about an event, a student, or a teacher at your school.

_____

_____

_____

_____

_____

_____

_____

_____

_____

Men and Women

Lesson A | How do I look?

1 Vocabulary Workout

A Unscramble the words for describing people.

1. cathtile   _____
2. snadhome   _____
3. lewl-tubli   _____
4. tttarcavie   _____

5. eettpi   _____
6. terpyt   _____
7. teelnag   _____
8. dabl   _____

B Write the words from **A** in the correct box.

Women	Men	Both

C Describe these people. Use words from **A** and other vocabulary you know.

①

1. _____
   _____
   _____
   _____
   _____

②

2. _____
   _____
   _____
   _____
   _____

2 Conversation Workout

(A) Number this conversation to put it in order.

_____ I don't think you should do that.

_____ Well, for one thing, it might look stupid.

___1___ Guess what? I'm going to shave my head.

_____ Shave your head? Why?

_____ I know. That's what everyone says.

_____ Because being bald is cool!

_____ Why not?

_____ For another, hair grows slowly. What happens if you change your mind?

(B) Now write new conversations using the expressions in the box.

> color my hair blue   first of all   second

1. Emi: _____

   You: _____

   Emi: _____

   You: _____

   Emi: _____

   You: _____

> change my name   in the first place   in the second

2. Walter: _____

   You: _____

   Walter: _____

   You: _____

   Walter: _____

3. Use your own idea.

   Your friend: _____

   You: _____

   Your friend: _____

   You: _____

   Your friend: _____

3 Language Workout

A It's 2:00 p.m. on Wednesday. Read Diane's list and write sentences with *already*, *just*, *still*, and *yet*.

> This week
> Monday
>   call Francisco
> ✓ buy present for Mom's
>   birthday
>
> Tuesday
> ✓ go to the bank
> ✓ get files from Stan
>   finish writing report
>
> Wednesday
> ✓ Mom's birthday—call her!
> ✓ 12:00 lunch with Carla and Yuki
>   answer e-mail
>   3:00 dentist appointment

Example: get files from Stan   *She's already gotten the files from Stan.*

1. (dentist appointment) _____

2. (present) _____

3. (report) _____

4. (Francisco) _____

5. (bank) _____

6. (lunch) _____

7. (call mother) _____

8. (e-mail) _____

B Complete the sentences with *still*, *yet*, **or** *already*.

1. In this class, we've learned several useful things _____.

2. Joe's boss is upset because he _____ hasn't finished typing all the letters.

3. I've _____ made my plane reservations. Now I'm going to call the hotel.

4. Have you started cooking dinner _____? It's almost 6:00 and I'm hungry.

5. I _____ haven't decided what to do tonight.

6. We've studied four units of this book _____. We _____ have eight more units to study.

7. Teresa doesn't know _____ what she wants to do after graduation.

8. This exercise looked difficult, but I've finished it _____.

C Write sentences about your activities today using these words.

1. (already) _____

2. (yet, not) _____

3. (just) _____

4. (still, not) _____

Men and Women

Lesson B | Dating

1 Vocabulary & Language Workout

A Fill in the spaces with a word from the box.

romantic	attracted	intelligence	sincere	looks
personality	common	casual	seeking	long-term

1. _____ is a very important quality for doctors, teachers, and engineers.

2. Eduardo and I have a lot of _____ interests. We both like sports, dancing, and going to old movies.

3. If you are _____, you are honest and say what you are really thinking.

4. Kate is _____ new tennis partners, so she joined a sports club.

5. A _____ relationship is one that continues for years.

6. I don't care if my boyfriend is handsome. For me, personality is more important than

   _____.

7. That movie is so _____! It's a love story about two people who meet in Paris.

8. A _____ relationship is not very serious—it's just for fun.

9. I'm _____ to smart women. I like to talk about books, movies, and ideas with my girlfriend.

10. My best friend has a wonderful _____. She's kind, caring, and fun to be with.

B Are these things important to you in a friend or date? Explain your reasons.

1. Intelligence is (very / a little bit / not) important to me because _____

   _____

2. Personality _____

3. Looks _____

4. Common interests _____

5. Sincerity _____

C Write the second word of the phrasal verb that means these things.

1. invite on a date	ask _____	
2. say no to an invitation	turn _____	
3. stop dating	break _____	with
4. meet without planning	run _____	
5. stop feeling sad about	get _____	
6. go on a date	go _____	with
7. have a good relationship	get _____	with
8. have another boyfriend or girlfriend	cheat _____	

A Read the newspaper article.

THE DAILY NEWS

8 JULY

Jason Chao is a modern guy. He works as an Internet technology consultant. He likes fast cars, fast computers, and making life faster in every way. "But to meet that special woman," Chao says, "I think the slow, old-fashioned way is best." Now, he meets prospective girlfriends through social clubs.

In the last ten years, many men and women have tried finding a partner over the Internet, through TV and radio shows, or planned events such as speed dating. But recently many single people have decided that it's better, and even easier, to meet dates without technology.

"The Internet has caused problems in dating," said Dr. Rachel Levine, a psychologist. "We think the Internet will help us find love a lot faster. But even if you have a great relationship online, you still have to meet face to face. And then the relationship often doesn't work."

For 26-year-old Carmen Torres, high-tech dating doesn't work, because you can't really judge things like looks, personality, and sincerity online, she said. "On the computer, a person can tell you all of their great qualities, and leave out the bad points. So you can waste a lot of time meeting guys that you really don't get along with."

Tina Gunderson, age 29, agreed. "I know Internet dating is really popular, but I've never tried it. I meet lots of guys through work, and friends, and living downtown," she said. "That starts a friendship a lot of times. And that often leads to happier, more relaxed dates."

B Write the letter of the answer on the line.

1. Carmen Torres thinks ____
   a. Internet dating is good for busy people.
   b. people don't tell the truth over the Internet.
   c. Internet dating is old-fashioned.
   d. personality is more important than looks.

2. Dr. Levine says ____
   a. you can meet a great boyfriend or girlfriend over the Internet.
   b. outgoing people don't need to use Internet dating.
   c. the Internet is the fastest way to find a good relationship.
   d. Internet relationships have problems when the people meet.

3. Tina Gunderson thinks ____
   a. people should be friends before they start dating.
   b. Internet dating will be more popular in the future.
   c. old-fashioned guys are very boring.
   d. she would like to try Internet dating.

4. The best title for this reading is: ____
   a. Why You Should Try Internet Dating.
   b. How Technology Has Changed Our Lives.
   c. How to Have a Happy Relationship.
   d. Going Back to Old Ways of Dating.

C Find and correct the spelling mistakes.

I think the best way to meet a boyfriend is at your job. You can get to know a person very well in a realaxed way, with no pressure, because you're not dateing. You can learn about his personallity because you spend a lot of time together. You will find out about his family, his interests, and his sense of humor. Best of all, you can ask other people's oppinion of him, and get advice from your freinds. I met my boyfriend at my ofice, and we're so happy togehter now!

D Write your ideas about the best way to meet a partner.

UNIT 5 Being Different

Lesson A | How to behave

1 Vocabulary Workout

A Write the opposite of these words.

1. usual   _un usual_   5. inoffensive   _offensive_
2. rude   _unrude_   6. typical   _atypical_
3. respectful   _disrespectful_   7. impolite   _polite_
4. appropriate _inappropriate_

B What do people in your country think about these things? Write them in the correct box. Then add more ideas of your own.

being late for an appointment	bringing a gift for your host	shaking hands
eating with chopsticks	bowing	wearing shorts
eating with a knife and fork	being late for a party	talking during dinner
smoking in front of your boss	wearing shoes inside a house	

Polite	eating with a knife and fork shaking hands
Rude	- being late for an appointment - smoking in front of your boss - being late for a party - wearing shorts
Typical	- talking during dinner
Unusual	- eating with chopsticks - bringing a gift for your host - bowing - wearing shoes inside a house

2 Conversation Workout

 A Cassie is going to have dinner with a host family in Japan. She asks her friend Tomoko about customs. Fill in Tomoko's answers.

> You should call and ask the family.   No, we usually sit on the floor.
> That's not polite. Try to eat just a little bit.   No problem. We use forks too.

Cassie: I can't speak Japanese very well. May I bring a friend to translate?
Tomoko: _You should call and ask the family._

Cassie: Can I sit on a chair?
Tomoko: _No, we usually sit on the floor._

Cassie: Is it okay if I say "no" to food I don't like?
Tomoko: _That's not polite. Try to eat a little bit._

Cassie: Is it all right to ask for a fork? I'm not very good with chopsticks.
Tomoko: _No problem. We use forks too._

B Now write new conversations about these places and customs.

1. A wedding—Saudi Arabia

   wear pants ☹   shake hands with the bride ☺
   dance at the party ☺   bring my boyfriend ☹

Mary: _I lik wearing pants. Can I wear pants in the wedding party?_
Fatima: _No, you can not we usually wear dresses._
Mary: _May I bring my boyfriend?_
Fatima: _No, it is a special party for women._
Mary: _How can I great the bride?_
Fatima: _You should shake hands with the bride?_
Mary: _Can I dance at the party?_
Fatima: _Yes, you can dance._

2. A holiday party—your country

Chris: _Can I wear Jenes in the holiday party?_
You: _No, you should wear Thob._
Chris: _How can I great People?_
You: _You can say "Ead Mubarik"._
Chris: _Can I bring my girlfriend?_
You: _No, but she can go to the ladies section._
Chris: _What can I eat or drink?_
You: _We eat meat and rice after drinking coffee._

A A foreign businessman is coming to work in your country. Complete the sentences with your own ideas. Use a gerund as subject.

Example: *Giving someone a present with your left hand is rude.*

1. In our country _shaking hands when you meet someone_ is polite.
2. _Maintaining eye contact when speaking to someone_ is important.
3. _Bringing a small gift when someone invite you_ is unusual.
4. _Wearing shorts in formal places._ is rude.
5. _Accepting someone invitation._ is appropriate.
6. _Chewing gum when you speak to someone_ is disrespectful.

B Now rewrite the sentences from **A**. Use *It + be + adjective + infinitive.*

Example: *It's rude to give someone a present with your left hand.*

1. In our country, it's _polite to shake hands when you meet someone._

2. It's _important to maintain eye contact when speaking to someone._

3. It's _unusual to bring a gift when someone invite you._

4. It's _rude to wear shorts in formal places._

5. It's _appropriate to accepte someone invitation._

6. It's _disrespectful to chew gum when you speak to someone._

C Write sentences with these words. Use the gerund or *It + be + adjective + infinitive.*

1. dangerous / drive very fast in bad weather
   It is dangerous to drive very fast in bad weather.

2. learn new words every day / important
   Learning new words every day is important.

3. expensive / eat in a restaurant every night
   It is expensive to eat in a restaurant every night.

4. study in a foreign country / not easy
   Studying in a foreign country isn't easy.

Being Different

Lesson B | Adjusting to a new place

1 Vocabulary & Language Workout

A Match the words with their meanings. Write the letter of the answer on the line.

1. environment _f_
2. customs _b_
3. regulations _h_
4. space _e_
5. talk _a_
6. habits _d_
7. barrier _g_
8. expression _c_

a. conversation
b. the habits in a country
c. the look on a person's face
d. things you always do

e. an empty area
f. the land, air, and place that you live in
g. a problem that stops people
h. rules or laws

B Estela is going to Toronto on a business trip. Look at her calendar.

MON	TUES	WED	THURS	FRI	SAT	SUN
10 Arrive Toronto, taxi to meeting 11 meeting 1 lunch with Al	8 breakfast meeting 10–3 factory tour evening: RELAX!	4 product presentation 7 company dinner		12 lunch with Mr. Carter afternoon write report	FREE TIME (shopping, movie . . .)	RELAX at hotel 2 fly home

Number the events 1, 2, or S (same time). Then write sentences two ways. Use *before, after, as soon as,* and *while*.

Example: have factory tour _2_   attend breakfast meeting _1_
Before she has the factory tour, she'll attend the breakfast meeting.
She'll have the factory tour after she attends the breakfast meeting.

1. give the product presentation _1_   attend the company dinner _2_
   Before she attends the breakfast meeting, she'll give the product presentation.
   She'll attend the company dinner after she gives the product presentation.

2. arrive in Toronto _S_   take a taxi to the meeting _S_
   She'll take a taxi to the meeting while she arriving in Toronto.
   As soon as she arrives in Toronto, she'll take a taxi to the meeting.

3. have lunch with Mr. Carter _1_   write her report _2_
   Before she writes her report, she'll have lunch with Mr. Carter.
   She'll write her report after she has lunch with Mr. Carter.

4. have free time _S_   go shopping _S_
   While having free time, she'll go shopping.
   She'll go shopping as soon as she has free time.

2 Reading & Writing

A **Read this article and number the paragraphs to put them in order. Write the number on the line.**

When people go to live in a new country, many of them experience culture shock—a feeling of being confused and worried in their new culture. Usually, culture shock has five stages, but some people don't experience all of them.

__2__   But then, the problems begin. Newcomers must deal with housing, transportation, study, work, and shopping, while they are learning to use a new language. They often feel extremely tired, sad, or depressed, because of the difficulty of understanding so many new things. This is the "culture shock" stage.

__1__   In the beginning, most people feel very excited. Everything around them is new and interesting, and people enjoy exploring their new culture. This is sometimes called the "honeymoon stage."

__5__   In the final stage, people feel at home in their new country. They have learned new habits and customs, and they now have friends and business associates. Their life has a new routine, at work or school, and they feel comfortable with it. This stage is called "integration."

__3__   After some time, people solve their everyday problems, like housing and shopping, and their language skills improve. They are able to communicate more with people of their host country, and they enjoy life more. This stage is called "initial adjustment."

__4__   After a longer time away from home, though, some people begin to feel lonely. They miss their family and friends, and they think that they will never have close friends in the new country. They can't talk about their feelings and emotions very well in the new language, so they feel sad and alone. This is the "mental isolation" stage.

B **Who said it? Write the name of the stage for each statement.**

1. "I can't understand these people. They talk so fast, and their customs are so strange. Every day I do something wrong and people laugh at me. Why did I come here?"
   Stage: _culture shock._

2. "This is such an interesting country! The food is great! I'm going to take language lessons and learn twenty new words every day. And I'm going sightseeing this weekend."
   Stage: _honeymoon_

3. "I know lots of people here, but I can't tell anyone about my problems. No one understands me. This language is so difficult. I'll never learn it."
   Stage: _mental isolation_

4. "I really love my job here. My coworkers are so friendly, and we talk about everything. Tomorrow I'm going to my boss's son's wedding. Weddings here are so beautiful!"
   Stage: _integration_

5. "Today I could understand the woman in the market. My listening is getting better. And now I know the names of all the foods, so I can ask for them."
   Stage: _initial adjustment_

C **Read this letter to the newspaper. Fill in the spaces with** *before, after, as soon as,* **or** *while.*

Here is some advice for people who want to study in France.
(1) _Before_ you come here, learn as much French as possible. (2) _As soon as_ you arrive here, start looking for an apartment right away. There aren't many cheap apartments here. (3) _After_ you find an apartment, you can buy furniture at the flea market or from other students.
(4) _While_ you're studying, you can also have a part-time job. You can find job announcements at your school. (5) _As soon as_ you see an announcement, you should call about the job. The good jobs are gone very fast!
(6) _While_ you are in France, be sure to take time for sightseeing and fun. It's a really interesting country.

D **Write advice for foreigners who come to your country to work or study.**

Here is some advice for people who want to work in Saudi Arabia. Before you come here, you should search online for hotels. As soon as you arrive in Saudi Arabia, start looking for an apartment. After you find an apartment, you can buy furniture at Alaoays because it has different shops and cheap. After you settle, you should buy a car because we do not have public transportation. While you are in Saudi Arabia, take a tour around. It is really interesting country.

1 Vocabulary Workout

A Solve this crossword puzzle with vocabulary from the lesson.

We're in Business

Across

2. ____ has the same meaning as "almost."

5. Sheep are ____ in Iceland.

10. Germany and Sweden ____ very good cars.

12. ____ has the same meaning as "about."

14. If you ____ people, you tell them what to do.

Down

1. to buy from another country

3. Many companies ____ their products on TV.

4. to plan and make a new product

6. If you ____ people, you give them a job.

7. This metal is used to make soda cans and airplane

8. a symbol for a company

9. The president's speech was ____ on radio and TV.

11. Companies ____ to make the most money.

13. ____ has the same meaning as "buy."

2 Conversation Workout

 A How much? How many? Circle the best answer.

1. The school has <u>approximately 400</u> students.

   a. 395   b. 520

2. The house cost <u>about $100,000</u>.

   a. $90,000   b. $102,000

3. The project took <u>nearly three months</u>.

   a. 11 weeks   b. 15 weeks

4. Our sales increased <u>over two percent</u> last year.

   a. 1.9%   b. 2.2%

5. You can save <u>up to 50%</u> if you buy now.

   a. 30%–50%   b. 50%–65%

 B A reporter is interviewing the director of a language school.
Complete the conversation by writing in the answers.

> Yes. The number of students increased over 10 percent last year.
> Now we have nearly 20.
> Approximately 500 people study here every month.
> The fee is about $100 per month.
> It's called Universal Institute.

Reporter: What's the name of your English school?
Director: _____

Reporter: How many students are there?
Director: _____

Reporter: And how many teachers do you have?
Director: _____

Reporter: How much does it cost to study at your school?
Director: _____

Reporter: Is your school growing?
Director: _____

 **C** Write an interview about your school. Use *about, approximately, over,*
or *nearly* if you don't know the exact number.

Reporter: _____
Director: _____
Reporter: _____
Director: _____
Reporter: _____
Director: _____
Reporter: _____
Director: _____
Reporter: _____
Director: _____

A Write the past participle of these verbs. Use your dictionary if necessary.

Examples: produce *produced*   speak *spoken*

1. start _____
2. build _____
3. teach _____
4. make _____
5. find _____
6. write _____

7. visit _____
8. do _____
9. send _____
10. cook _____
11. read _____
12. eat _____

"Cheer up! Success is built upon a lot of failure."

B Change these sentences to passive. Pay attention to past and present.

1. The Smith Corporation employs two hundred people.

   _____

2. Teams in many countries play baseball.

   _____

3. Frank typed the letters.

   _____

4. Over one billion people speak Chinese.

   _____

5. Two women wrote that book.

   _____

6. Farmers in Mexico grow excellent coffee.

   _____

C Fill in the correct form of the verb, active or passive.

1. Portuguese _____ in Brazil and Portugal. (**speak**)
2. Every year, thousands of tourists _____ the pyramids in Egypt. (**visit**)
3. Our homework _____ by the teacher every week. (**check**)
4. People across East Asia _____ Chinese New Year. (**celebrate**)
5. Nowadays, English _____ by more and more children in elementary school. (**learn**)
6. Wood _____ in many different products, like paper and furniture. (**use**)
7. The sports club _____ uniforms for all its members. (**provide**)
8. The month of Ramadan _____ in Islamic countries. (**celebrate**)
9. Stamps _____ at the post office. (**sell**)
10. My parents _____ my new hairstyle. (**hate**)
11. Mr. Kim always _____ the newspaper on the bus to work. (**read**)
12. Banana trees _____ in warm, sunny climates. (**find**)

Big Business

Lesson B | The ABCs of advertising

1 Vocabulary & Language Workout

A Unscramble the kinds of advertising.

1. llibdroab _____
2. churorbe _____
3. stoper _____
4. permbu rickets _____

5. kyingwrits _____
6. downiw splidya _____
7. knuj lami _____
8. VT mercmiloca _____

B Do you pay attention to these kinds of advertising? Write them in the chart below. Add three more kinds.

Yes, often.	Yes, sometimes.	No.

C Look at the picture. Write sentences with *because, so,* **and** *although.* **You need to add more words.**

Example: Pete talked on his cell phone   didn't look at the road
Because Pete talked on his cell phone, he didn't look at the road.

1. car crashed   tree was destroyed

_____

2. woman angry   shout at Pete

_____

3. woman angry   tree was killed

_____

4. said "I'm really sorry"   woman yelled louder

_____

5. Pete unhappy   car was damaged

_____

6. car was damaged   could still drive it

_____

A • **Read the article.**

A Different Kind of Holiday

Advertising is everywhere. It's on race cars and subway trains, on T-shirts and billboards. Every day, you see hundreds of ads, and each advertiser wants you to buy their product. But do we really need all these products?

A group in Canada says "No." In 1991, they started an event called Buy Nothing Day, to protest against **consumerism** and waste. Every year, on the last Friday in November, no one should spend any money for 24 hours. The event has **spread** to over 15 countries around the world, including Japan, Australia, and the United Kingdom.

In the United States, Buy Nothing Day takes place on the Friday after the Thanksgiving holiday. This is usually the busiest day of the year in department stores and shopping malls. Traditionally, it's the first day of the Christmas shopping season, when Americans buy gifts for family and close friends.

However, this "season" has grown longer every year. Now some stores put up their Christmas window displays in the middle of October, and Americans are **pressured** to buy gifts for every one of their relatives, for all of their coworkers, and for everyone they do business with. Many people feel that they are forgetting the real **significance** of the holidays, because companies just want them to spend more money.

Of course, Buy Nothing Day **supporters** don't want to change just one day. They want the change to continue all year. But if we take a break from shopping on one day, we can start thinking about what we really need in life. Michael Smith, British organizer of Buy Nothing Day, says: "Our message is clear: shop less, live more!"

B • **Find the words in bold in the reading with these meanings.**

1. moved to more places   _____

2. meaning   _____

3. people who agree with something _____

4. pushed to do something   _____

5. spending money to buy happiness _____

C Answer the questions with information from the reading.

1. What is the name of this event? _____

2. What should people do then? _____

3. Where is this day celebrated? _____

4. Where did it start? _____

5. What also happens in the United States on that day? _____

6. Why don't some Americans like Christmas shopping? _____

7. What do the organizers want to change? _____

D Fill in the spaces with *although, because,* **or** *so.*

I saw a cute commercial for Barko Dog Food on TV. It's about a fat old dog who can talk. In the beginning, he's sleeping. Then he smells something, **(1)** _____ he gets up. He says, "Mmm, it smells like steak!" He starts looking for the steak **(2)** _____ he's hungry. He goes in the living room, and in the dining room, and he says, "Where's the steak? Where's the steak?" **(3)** _____ he looks everywhere, he can't find the steak. Finally, he goes in the kitchen. His owner has just opened a can of Barko, and the dog says, "It's STEAK!" I really like this commercial **(4)** _____ the dog's voice is so funny.

E Write about a TV commercial that you like or don't like. What is it about? Why do/don't you like it?

_____

_____

_____

_____

_____

_____

_____

_____

_____

_____

_____

_____

_____

Language Summaries

Unit 1 *Indoors and Outdoors*

Lesson A

Vocabulary Link

air conditioner
alarm clock
barbecue grill
burglar alarm
can opener
frying pan
remote control
smoke detector
swimming pool
vacuum cleaner
washing machine

Language Link

Describing use: *be used to* +
infinitive; *be used for* + gerund
or noun

Speaking Strategy

Useful Expressions:
Saying what you want

I need a lot of space.
I want to live on a houseboat.
I'd like/love to have a house with
  20 rooms.

Lesson B

Vocabulary Link

bus station
campus
newspaper stand
park
parking meter
parking space
subway entrance
taxi stand
traffic light

Language Link

Expressing prohibition

Unit 2 *Life Is All About Change*

Lesson A

Vocabulary Link

adolescence
adult
adulthood
childhood
grown-up
infancy
infant
middle-aged
senior citizen
teenager
youth

Language Link

Future forms

Speaking Strategy

Useful Expressions:
Expressing intentions

I'm planning to + verb
I'm going to + verb
I plan/intend to + verb
I'm thinking about + verb + *ing*

Lesson B

Vocabulary Link

fall in love
get divorced
get married
get promoted
graduate
have a baby
move out
retire

Language Link

Modals of future possibility

Unit 3 *Newspapers and the News*

Lesson A

Vocabulary Link

cartoonist
copyeditor
critic
international correspondent
journalist
news anchor
photographer
publisher

Language Link

Describing people with
prepositional and
participial phrases

Speaking Strategy

**Useful Expressions:
Asking about identity**

Who is Pat Rich?
Do you know Pat Rich?
Is that Pat Rich?
Do you know Pat Rich?
Can you tell me who Pat Rich is?

Lesson B

Vocabulary Link

comics
daily *(adv.)*
headlines
horoscope
publish *(v.)*
scan *(v.)*
sections
sensational *(adj.)*
subscribe *(v.)*
weather forecast

Language Link

Review of the present perfect

Unit 4 *Men and Women*

Lesson A

Vocabulary Link

athletic
attractive
bald
elegant
handsome
petite
pretty
well built

Language Link

The present perfect with *already,
just, never, still*, and *yet*

Speaking Strategy

**Useful Expressions:
Giving more than one reason**

For one thing, . . . For another, . . .
In the first place, . . . In the second, . . .
First of all, . . . Second of all, . . .

Lesson B

Vocabulary Link

attracted to
casual
common
intelligence
long-term relationship
looks
personality
romantic
seeking
sincere

Language Link

Introduction to phrasal verbs

Language Summaries

Unit 5 Being Different

Lesson A

Vocabulary Link

appropriate
atypical
disrespectful
impolite
inappropriate
inoffensive
offensive
polite
respectful
typical
unusual
usual

Language Link

It + be + adjective + infinitive;
gerund as subject

Speaking Strategy

Useful Expressions:
Asking about rules

Can I . . . ?
May I . . . ?
Is it all right/OK to . . . ?
Is it all right/OK if I . . . ?

Lesson B

Vocabulary Link

eating habits
facial expressions
holiday customs
language barrier
personal space
physical environment
small talk
traffic regulations

Language Link

Future time clauses with *before, after, as soon as, when,* and *while*

Unit 6 Big Business

Lesson A

Vocabulary Link

advertise
compete
develop
employ
manage
produce
purchase
ship

Language Link

The passive voice: the simple present and the simple past

Speaking Strategy

Useful Expressions:
Talking about approximate amounts

Approximately 400 employees
   work here.
The average worker earns **about**
   $20,000 per year.
We have **a large number of**
   opportunities to expand our business.
We spent **nearly** three months on
   the project.
Our profits will decline **over** two
   percent this year.
You can save **up to** 50% if you buy
   it now.

Lesson B

Vocabulary Link

billboard
brochure
bumper sticker
junk mail
poster
skywriting
TV commercial
window display

Language Link

Connecting words: *because, so, although*

Grammar Notes

Unit 1 *Indoors and Outdoors*

Lesson A

Language Link: Describing use—*be used* + infinitive; *be used for* + gerund or noun

You can use these three structures to talk about how an object is used:

be used + infinitive:
> That machine **is used** *to dry* dishes. It only takes 90 seconds.

be used for + gerund:
> This strange-looking object **is used** *for* **cooking**

be used for + noun:
> A helmet is used *for* **protection**.

Lesson B

Language Link: Expressing prohibition

- *Not allowed to* and *can't* are commonly used to state prohibition when speaking:
    > There's **no smoking allowed** in this office building.
    > I'm sorry, but you **aren't allowed to** smoke here. Please step outside.
    > You **can't** enter the studio now. They're recording.

- *No* + gerund is used on signs to show something is prohibited:
    > No smoking.
    > No fishing.

- *Mustn't* can express a strong warning. It is more common to use *can't* in spoken English.
    > You **mustn't** drink and drive.

Unit 2 *Life Is All About Change*

Lesson A

Language Link: Future forms

Will is used . . .
• for general predictions.
• when you decide something at the moment of speaking.

Be going to is used . . .
• for general predictions.
• for future plans and intentions.
• for when you know something is about to happen.

The present continuous is used . . .
• for future plans that have already been made.

The simple present is used . . .
• for fixed schedules in the future

Lesson B

Language Link: Modals of future possibility

	Modals of future possibility
Is she going to retire next year?	She **may/might/could.**
Will you be late?	I **may/might/could (be).**
Are you going to attend the party?	They **may/might not.** I'm not feeling well.
When do you start school?	I'm not sure. I **may/might/could** start on Tuesday or Wednesday.

- Use *may, might,* or *could* to talk about future possibility.

- Use the negative form (not contracted) of *may* or *might* to express negative future possibility. Don't use the negative form of *could.*

Unit 3 *Newspaper and the News*

Lesson A

Language Link: Describing people with prepositional and participial phrases

Describing people with prepositional and participial phrases
prepositional phrase   She's the news anchor with straight black hair.   • Examples of prepositions are *in, on,* and *with.* A prepositional phrase includes a preposition and a noun (*woman*) or pronoun (*one*).   • The prepositional phrase follows the noun it is modifying.   • Use the definite article *the* (*the news anchor*) when the speaker and listener are thinking about the same person.
participial phrases   They're the couple sitting on the sofa.   He's the one taking photographs.   • A present participle is a verb + *-ing.* It also follows the noun it is modifying.

Lesson B

Language Link: Review of the present perfect

- Use the present perfect for actions that began in the past and continue in the present:
  I'm a reporter at *The Daily News.* I**'ve worked** here for three years.

- You can also use the present perfect to talk about actions that happened in the past when the time they happened isn't important:
  Have you ever **read** this magazine?

- We use the present perfect with *just* for an action that has been completed recently:
  I**'ve** just **finished** with the newspaper. You can borrow it now

Unit 4 *Men and Women*

Lesson A

Language Link: The present perfect with *already, just, never, still,* **and** *yet*

- Use *yet* in questions and negative sentences for things that have not been finished at the present moment:
  They haven't gotten married **yet**. / They haven't **yet** gotten married.

- Use *already* in affirmative sentences to say you've completed something. Questions with *already* can indicate surprise that the action has been completed:
  I've **already** finished it. / I've finished it **already**.
  Have you **already** finished your homework? That was fast!

- Use *just* for an action that happened a short time in the past:
  We've **just** met.

- Use *never* for actions that did not happen at any time in the past:
  He's **never** been well built.

- Use *still* in negative sentences to indicate something hasn't happened yet. In the affirmative, *still* typically occurs with tenses other than the present perfect:
  She **still** hasn't called him.
  She's **still** attending college.
  They're **still** married.

- In spoken American English, we can sometimes substitute the simple past for the present perfect with no change in meaning:
  Have you *finished* **yet**? = *Did* you finish yet?

Lesson B

Language Link: Introduction to phrasal verbs

Verb	Phrasal Verb
I **asked** her a question.	I **asked** her **out** on a date.
She **turned** the key and opened the lock.	It hurts to be **turned down**.
The kids **go** to school by bus.	Let's **go out** to dinner.

- Phrasal verbs are made up of two or three words.

- They are composed of a verb and a particle (a preposition or adverb).

- Common particles are *out, up, off,* and *down*. The particle can change the meaning of the verb phrase.

Unit 5 *Being Different*

Lesson A

Language Link: *It + be* + adjective + infinitive; gerund as subject

- *It + be* + adjective + infinitive sentences can have the same meaning as sentences that use the gerund as subject:
  Having a cup of coffee after dinner **is customary.** = **It's customary to have** a cup of coffee after dinner.

- Gerunds (*-ing* forms), as the subjects of sentences, act like nouns. The verb following the gerund takes the third-person singular form:
  Swimming is fun.
  Learning English is difficult.

Lesson B

Language Link: Future time clauses with *before, after, as soon as, when,* and *while*

- Future time clauses contain a main clause and a time clause. The time clause can come before or after the main clause. Notice the comma:
  When I get home, I'll call you.
  I'll call you **when I get home.**

- In clauses with *after, when,* and *as soon as* the event in the main clause happens after the event in the time clause:
  After I get up, I'll take a shower. (1st event = get up)
  When I start attending my new school, I'll try to make new friends. (1st event = start attending school)
  I'll go to my hotel **as soon as I arrive.** (1st event = arrive)

- In clauses with *before* the event in the main clause happens first:
  Before I move to the U.S., I'll study English so I can communicate. (1st event = study English)

- In clauses with *while* the events in both clauses happen at the same time:
  I'll probably get homesick **while I'm living overseas.**

- Don't use *will* in both the time clause and the main clause. Use it in the main clause only.

- Use the simple present as future in the time clause.

Unit 6 *Big Business*

Lesson A

Language Link: The passive voice—the simple present and the simple past

Tense	The passive voice
Simple Present:	English **is (not) spoken** in the office. Our products **are (not) advertised** on the Internet.
Simple Past:	The company **was (not) sold** in 1999. New software **was (not) developed** for this computer.

- The subject of a passive verb corresponds to the object of an active verb:

Active Voice	Passive Voice
object	subject
Our company **produces** cars.	Cars **are produced** by our company.

- We can use *by* + **noun** if we need or want to show who performs an action:
  Yahoo was founded *by two students.*

Lesson B

Language Link: Connecting words—*because, so, although*

- Connecting words "connect" two clauses. They show the relationship in meaning between the two clauses.

- **Although** is used to connect two contrasting statements. It introduces a statement that makes the main statement seem surprising:
  Although/Even though it's on sale, I'm not going to buy it.
  I'm not going to buy it **although/even though** it's on sale.

- **Because** is used to show a reason. It answers *why* questions:
  I like the new cell phones **because** they are smaller and more convenient.
  Because they are smaller and more convenient, I like the new cell phones.

- **So** is used to show a result. It connects two main statements and is preceded by a comma:
  The new product didn't sell well, **so** the company lost money on it.

Answers

Page 6, 7. Communication, Activity A

The Self-Propelled Shoe

Toyota Motor Corporation has created a self-propelled shoe, which the carmaker says is the world's smallest motor vehicle. Its rear-wheel drive format uses two electric motors, one in the heel of each shoe, which allows for speeds up to 20 km (12 miles) per hour. The shoe was shown at Tokyo's Idea Expo, which features creative inventions by Toyota's employees that might be used 20 years in the future.

The Electrolux Trilobite

The Electrolux Trilobite is a robot vacuum cleaner. It goes around objects and under furniture. It automatically adjusts to bare floors or any heights of carpet. It even recharges itself. It makes vacuuming by hand a thing of the past.

The Bowlingual Translator

The Bowlingual Translator is an innovative device that translates a dog's barks and growls into human language. It was first sold in Japan but is now available in other countries. It can translate for more than 80 different kinds of dogs. Japanese Prime Minister Junichiro Koizumi gave Russian President Vladimir Putin two Bowlingual Translators, one for each of his dogs.

Page 59, 6. Language Link, Activity C.

The company is Yahoo!

Page 69, 6. The Taj Mahal and Ayer's Rock, Activity B

Answers: **A.** (Ayer's Rock)–2, 3, 5, **B.** (The Taj Mahal)–1, 4, 6, 7